7 INVESTMENTS IN YOUR 20'S THAT WILL CHANGE YOUR LIFE

BRIDGING THE WEALTH GAP

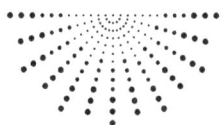

DAN SARVER

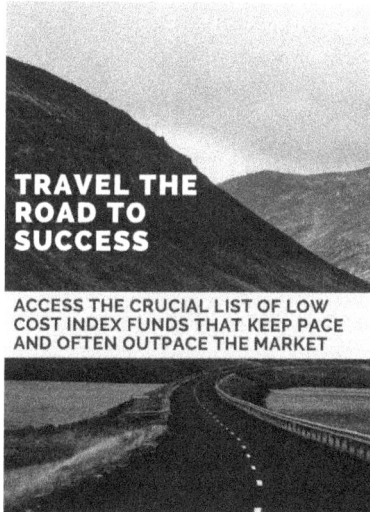

TRAVEL THE ROAD TO SUCCESS

ACCESS THE CRUCIAL LIST OF LOW COST INDEX FUNDS THAT KEEP PACE AND OFTEN OUTPACE THE MARKET

Free Gift to Readers

Access the exclusive list of the nine lowest cost index funds backed by Vanguard, Fidelity, and others. You don't want to miss out on these nine blue-chip investments! Visit the link below to get yours instantly.

https://danbusinesslifestyle.activehosted.com/f/5

CONTENTS

7 INVESTMENTS IN YOUR 20'S THAT WILL CHANGE YOUR LIFE

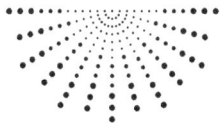

INTRODUCTION

How do you make money at a young age so you can enjoy luxuries later in life?

This question began to gnaw at my heart as I turned nineteen. I became sensitive to my environment. I began to reflect on the lives of the people around me. A few older people I associated with were wealthy, but more than half of the older adults I associated with were struggling. It was clear that whoever had money at old age didn't work for it at old age. They certainly worked for it in their youth. Whoever was poor might owe it to their youth too.

At first, I assumed the poor guys were the lazy ones. But I was utterly wrong and discovered that was a stereotyped fallacy. Many people whose finances declined at old age were not always poor from the start. They were splendid men, sensational women, and gleaming people who worked hard for their money.

Oddly enough, that story was different for most people who had an abundance of money at old age. They were hardly rich in their youths. They were mostly people who earned average pay, like the group above. They hardly lived flashy lives or outstepped their average earnings. But they certainly took a smart step to build wealth that everyone else didn't. And it all happened in their youth. What was it?

I dreamed someday I would invite these two classes of people and question them in a debate; what happened in your 20's?

As luck would have it, I didn't need that debate to find the missing jigsaw puzzle. I discovered that answer through studying the financial habits of people around me and through years of ambitious research. Through high school, I was fascinated with the idea of how a person can build long-term wealth. I was determined to find a step by step process modeling wealth and success. You will find the answer in this book. It is not rocket science, brain surgery, or something entirely out of this world to comprehend. It is a simple act; Investment. What happened in the wealthy man's youth was clear. The wealthy man began investing in his youth. The poor man saved or did nothing.

As children, we learn almost every piece of information from three places. Our family, friends, and school. As children, our friends didn't know anything about finances. Hopefully, our families gave us some pointers on money management. Lastly, the public education system never prepared its students for wealth building. The public school system never said a word about investments, let alone a formula to build long-term wealth.

At this point, I didn't know how to build wealth either.

I thought I would work my entire life, save enough, set up a pension plan, and enjoy my declining years in the quietest parts of the country. But that reality changed when I met an elderly woman who taught me how to structure my financial life.

From her series of lessons, it became evident that we shared the same dream as teenagers. Most people all share the same dream to a degree. You are probably thinking about it too.

We all want freedom. In its broadest context, everyone around the world wants to increase their level of freedom. Types of freedoms include physical, spiritual, national, state, and financial.

She retired as she desired, but she still wanted a good life. She still wanted the luxuries and splendors that life could offer. She wanted to be financially independent. Her meager pension was not going to afford it. It was no different from her past. It seemed she received meager salaries just to keep her body and soul as one. She soon became heartbroken. That wasn't the plan!

In addition, the economy wasn't helping matters. The economy is fast revolving in a manner that $1,000 today, cannot afford what you could have had with $1,000 ten years ago. So, the money she saved was just not valued enough to meet her modern needs.

Where does that leave her? Where will the rat race of life leave you?

Saving money with a bank is not the way to the promised land. There is one way to guarantee wealth at old age; *Invest in your 20's.*

What is investing? How does it work? How much money do you need to invest? Will there be setbacks? What is the safest method of investing?

There is a lot to discuss...

To be frank with you, the world of investing can be overwhelming. There are many things to know and numerous turns to take. It also depends on who you ask. There are several ways to be an investor. Investments mean something different to everyone. It can be very complicated on your own. You may get frustrated before you even get started.

More than half of the people who want to invest will quit at some point. My empirical research has suggested that up to 30% of people make the wrong investment choices too. Most of them lose and quit within a few years.

However, these statistics should not turn you off from the idea of investing and changing your life. Your future self will thank you. As long as you pay close attention to the seven suggested investment options in the following chapters, I can assure you a groundbreaking success in your future financial situation.

I have tried out many different investments over the years. I have risked a whopping amount of my earnings in a few investments. It is not a surprise that I have lost, and I have won. As the saying goes, there have been good days, and there sure have been horrible ones. But good days and bad days do not matter. Long-term success is the focus of this book.

During my exploration, I became fascinated by seven *special* categories of investments. I noticed how reliable and promising they are when compared to others. Then, I focused all of my efforts on them. Anyone willing to put 20% of their earnings into a portfolio with these seven invest-ments alone will become a millionaire. Not overnight, not in five years, nor ten. If you invest part of your monthly earn-ings in structured long-term investments as a 20-year-old, the sky is the limit. Anyone in their 20's has a tremendous advantage because time is on their side.

If you are between the age of 20 and 30-years-old, trust me when I tell you that you are not going to miss the 20% you put away towards your investments. Investing 20% of your earnings into your future is the greatest cause you can donate to. Your future self, spouse, and children will thank you.

If you are skeptical, it should only be because I am not a fifty-year-old guru or a millionaire yet, but I am a young man striving for financial independence. What is financial independence?

"The ability to live from the income of your own personal resources."

— JIM ROHN

I would have to agree and add financial independence is having enough income, from your investments and passive businesses, to pay for your living expenses for the rest of your life without relying on traditional employment. I doubt a traditional job can bring that degree of assurance.

So, if you are in your 20's or early 30's, investing may be the wager you've got to stick to. I have pledged to show you the industry secrets of investing that the public education system didn't want you to know growing up. Rather than the rich getting richer, let us strive for the poor to get wealthier. I will answer your burning questions about investments and how it works. I will reveal every bit of information you need to know about building long-term wealth by the end of this book.

Seriously?

Yes. I am neither the lord of currency nor something close to that. But I have seen enough to understand how investing in the stock market can change a person's life for the better. There are statistically proven strategies and a few tricks when picking the right investments. They will be debunked in this book. I honestly think you will be stunned. Being financially independent in twenty five years is mind-blowing for someone in their 20's or 30's but very realistic in the world of investors.

If you stick to my suggestions in this guide, your understanding of financial investments will go through the roof. You do not have to use all seven investment categories, but it is strongly advised that you try more than one.

You may retire much earlier than you had planned. It means you can spend more days with your family, more tee time on the golf course, and traveling the world as you've always wanted without worrying about the health of your finances. The important thing is to stay glued. I hope you will find these investment theories easy to adopt. And I hope you will abide by the process come hell or high water. If you are not willing to sacrifice for your goals, your goals will become your sacrifice.

PART I
THE BIG PICTURE

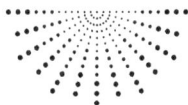

1

ACHIEVING LIFELONG DREAMS

From the early stages of my youth, I have never forgotten that I will grow old someday. I always bear in mind that someday I will grow tired and be unable to take up a serious job anymore. I want to be a good grandfather. The wealthy grandpa that flies to Venice with his grandchildren and stuff them with sugar and goodies. Their parents can deal with that when they get back home. When I finally decide to hang my career boots, I want to have enough resources to travel anywhere and afford nice things.

If I keep working at old age, it should merely be because I wasn't ready to sit with the kids at home and fight over the TV remote control. I know it is conventionally difficult to be set for financial independence and live "the good life", but living "the good life" was exactly what I wanted—my *dream*.

Comparatively, your dreams might be something similar. You might be doing all you can to become stinkingly rich in as little time as possible. You might be pursuing the kind of wealth that will never dry up or dissolve the instant you stop working. Your dreams can be anything. I have no idea what you have chosen to do or not to do with your life.

Notwithstanding, I strongly assume that everyone wants to live their life in luxury and extravagance. No one wants to worry about how much money is left over after buying groceries and the rent is paid. We all want wealth to be available, whether we work, or stop working. It is a fair request for everyone who struggles through their youth and tries to make a buck anywhere they can find it.

The unsettling fact is that everyone does not attain these dreams. Some men and women depend on their children for daily survival. Many more live on social security, which scarcely affords anything. I should remind you that all of them were once like you. They had this zest about them and everyday when the walked outside their front door they would chase their dreams. But achieving it is not for everyone. It belongs to a group of people that you can join by reading the next few lines and acting them out.

If you are in your 20's and 30's, you have a high chance of achieving the dream of financial independence. Regardless of your circumstances, you can make financial decisions that will last a lifetime. You can retain enough money, make smart choices, and remain wealthy for the rest of your life. You will be able to achieve financial independence with no regrets. You will be able to walk out of your tiring job and for once, never look back with financial regret. You can create extra time for your family and friends while building wealth in your sleep.

Ideally, you will have enough time for relationships, passions, hobbies, wellness, and so on. It also means that as you grow into old age with your peers, you will likely grow healthier than most of them. Because you are not as stressed, you will look younger and happier. By your decisions, you direct your future.

Is this really possible? Am I dangling a fantasy before your eyes?

No way, it is absolutely possible and feasible to retire before your friends and colleagues. You will turn out to be wealthier than those who had higher-paying jobs and fatter salaries. It is easy and straightforward. All you need to do is invest. Invest?

Yes. You have to invest. Investment is the act of buying assets that are not going to be consumed today. You are investing so you can sell or reap the benefits from your investments in the future. If you consider that definition, you might presuppose that buying land and property is *the big investment*. You are along the right lines. But there is a lot more than that in the world of investment. Realistically, investing in land and houses (Real Estate Investment) is only a small portion of possibilities the world of investing offers. You will learn about the seven most profitable investments that can seal a wealthy future for you in the coming pages.

You should know, becoming a serious investor is not a cakewalk. It is not for people who long to be mollycoddled in the business world. It can be dangerous, wild, and full of surprising cut-corners. We might also say that it is not for people who hope to be treated fairly at all times. Yet, it remains the smartest and most sure way to get rich. The fact that investing is the smartest way to live in prosperity is why you should learn about it.

I have bounded myself to show you how to navigate these seven investments, without holding a thing back. We will rip it right from the roots and uncover the tricks and know-how. You will discover outcomes that pay you back instead of outcomes that take from you.

However, I need to prepare you before exposing these industry tricks. There are certain things about you that you have to adjust before successful investing can work for you. They will not only help you create financial independence, but they will also help you to believe it, chase it, and achieve it. You do not have to adjust your thought process if you already have an investment mindset. Just in case you don't, we will go over the *elements you must alter in your life before pursuing financial independence.*

- **Mindset**

Our mindset is the biggest asset we have as humans. The instant your mind assumes something is possible, it clings to it, and longs to make it happen. Vice versa. The instant you believe something is impossible, your subconscious will take your word for it. When I get into the details of these investments, some of them might sound completely incredulous. Some of them might look insane and farfetched, but you will understand them if your mind clings to an investment mindset.

"The brain has a powerful way of attracting things that are in harmony with it, good and bad."

— IDOWU KOYENIKAN

If you still doubt whether you can really retire before

your grey hair, you might have a tough time achieving it. Your day time job or a load of responsibilities should not hamper your lifelong goals. You have to stop asking if it is possible. You need to tell your mind that long-term investing is the solution.

Start seeing that there has to be some way to remain wealthy even when your job stops. There are smart decisions that can put you ahead of everyone else. You need to alter your mindset and stop wondering if it is possible. It is entirely possible, and your duty is to pursue it.

"Once your mindset changes, everything will change along with it."

— STEVE MARABOLI

I am going to recommend a lot of things to you in the following pages. There are several sacrifices to make, and they will all benefit you in the long run. But I have to make it clear that you will find it hard to make these sacrifices if you are not sure you can really achieve your financial dream. If you are able to follow my guide despite having a skeptical mindset, you will not be surprised by your future accomplishments.

"If your mindset is defeated, the results will be the same no matter how often you put up a physical fight."

— MAC DUKE

You can stop reading this book, close the pages, and go to sleep. I don't mind. But if you are going to keep reading, you need to believe that you can do this even if you don't have a financial background. Brace yourself. You are about to uncover a surprisingly simple way of growing your financial empire, and you must not doubt your process.

"Financial independence is a mindset before it is an action. Therefore, if you can change a mindset, the actions follow almost naturally."

— BRANDON TURNER (THE REAL ESTATE
CHAMPION)

- **Attitude and effort**

If you are aiming to become successful, making effort is a sine qua non (essential) for you. It is as simple as a *car illustration*. The illustration suggests that you have a world-class car sitting in your garage. That car will remain on that spot until you start the engine and move it. No matter the potential you have lying around you, you cannot manifest it if you don't add effort to it.

"It is only through labor and painful effort, by grim energy and resolute courage, that we move on to better things."

— THEODORE ROOSEVELT

This effort may vary. But you have to be up for taking the necessary strides to get to the finish line. As proof of this, the first way to prepare for the future is to accumulate funds. I mean, you will need much more than the necessary amount you are spending on your family each month. This suggests that you have to work extra hard till you have some more money lying around. It can be tiring and cumbersome. The saddening news is that it is either you put that extra effort in, or drop the idea of a bright future at the end of the tunnel.

"Financial peace isn't the acquisition of stuff. It's learning to live on less than you make, so you can give money back and have money to invest. You can't win until you do."

— DAVE RAMSEY

At this point, I am not sure about the sort of efforts that will be demanded of you. You may have to work overtime, take up an extra job, et cetera. You might also have to part way with some of the luxuries you enjoy at the moment. Brace up. Fierce times are approaching.

"We all have dreams. But in order to make dreams come into reality, it takes an awful lot of determination, dedication, self-discipline, and effort."

— JESSE OWENS

- **Financial management skills**

Research has proven that more than 70% of Americans do not keep a personal record of their finances. They remember that they pay bills and insurances. They are sure that they receive salaries. They also keep ideas of what they bought or sold in their head. And that is precisely where it all ends, in their heads.

Do you keep a financial record? What the average person does not know is that keeping a financial record is enough to give them direction. It is enough to help you guide your choices, and it can help you from spending lavishly while keeping pace for the future.

We mark down financial transactions at work. We know whether the company we are working for is making profits or going downhill. But strangely, we refuse to connect the dots that we are like companies ourselves. We receive income and make expenditures. We spend on basic amenities the way a company spends on salaries. If you make $2000 a month, for example, you should be able to document how you spent every penny of that paycheck. You should be able to predict how much you will have when the year ends, among other features of financial management and record-keeping. This should be way easier for wage earners. Para-doxically, they are the first class of people who pay little attention to financial records. They assume the record is set for them since they receive a fixed pay. And so they keep the records of their expenses and prospects in their head.

Let's get straight to the point. You cannot monitor your flow of income if you do not keep a financial record. You might be sure that you are receiving a steady income, but you will never be able to plan for the long-term.

"If money management is not something you enjoy, consider my perspective. I look at managing my money as if it were a part-time job. The time you spend monitoring your finances will pay off. You can make real money by cutting expenses and earning more interest on savings and investment. I'd challenge you to find a part-time job where you could potentially earn as much money for just an hour or two of your time."

— LAURA D. ADAMS

• Targets

What were your targets before you started reading this book? What were your aspirations?

More often than not, every person has specific aspirations. It might be gigantic or tiny, it could be casual or unusual, but the essential point is that everyone has a mental picture of what they want to be. I have no idea what yours is, but I can make a smart guess that it is a short-term ambition. Likely, they are targets that can be achieved in 6 months to three years. You are aiming to drive a sports car, own some type of estate, or get promoted at your job.

Have I just described you?

Congratulations. You have plans. They are only too little to reckon with your future. They are plans that hardly include your middle and old age. They are plans that spark up temporary enjoyment and give few clues about the future. That perspective must improve from this moment on. You have to begin to set more significant targets. Think about your current age. Then think about the next ten years. Estimate how much you want to be worth. Do not estimate alone, begin to work towards achieving that moment.

It is difficult to save for old age when you can get a cool car you have always admired. You will be tempted to spend more and save less but you should remember this crucial fact. It will be equally hard to save for the future if the present is your priority.

By way of illustration, let us say you earn $7,000 a month, and you desire a $40,000 car in the next couple of years. It is not farfetched, and it can undoubtedly be achieved. You will only have to save a massive chunk of your monthly earnings before you can afford it.

However, I want you to remember some facts; this is a short-term plan. You can achieve it in a year or two, with judicious savings. Short-term aspirations continue to temp every human mindset. It is not going to end with this vehicle. You are bound to desire something else before, or as soon as you get the car. If it is not a car, it is a leisure spa day. If it is not a modern dress, it is a gold chain or a Rolex. We have short-term aspirations all the time. If you continue to strive for the short-term, you will never have enough for the long-term. Therefore, you must learn not to give precedence to the temptations of short-term thinking. If you have a long-term investment that requires $500 each month, it has to be your priority against a cool car right now. *My take.*

꒰ ꒱

ENDING THOUGHTS

R ight from this moment, you should no longer make short-term targets your priority. You must begin to envision the long-term. Begin to transition your financial decisions towards the invisible future. As I have said earlier, I cannot be sure about your desire for the far future. But it is more than likely that you have long-term dreams you want to craft into your reality. If you still have no plans for the future, that has to be your starting assignment. You might have to take a coffee break, think about the long-term, and set yourself up for substantial aspirations first.

It should be clear at this point. You are not thrashing your short-term aspirations. It is entirely wrong to suffer so much for a future you may not grow to see. But it is equally wrong to live long in agony and difficulty. I will not fly to Venice with my future grandchildren if I do not have the funds to do so. So, you are lining up your short-term targets alongside your long-term targets. You are not abandoning your short-term aspirations. Instead, you are choosing to make your long-term aspirations your priority. When you begin to think that way, you will be influenced in no small measure. You will pull strings in your budget, finances, planning, and financial management, and you will be on the path to your version of a successful future.

Are you making an effort to understand the longevity of your long-term decisions? At this point in time, I hope you have the aspiration to achieve your life long dreams.

2

MINDSET FOR LONG-TERM WEALTH

"The rich invest their money and spend what is left, the poor spend their money and invest what is left."

— JIM ROHM

As I have pointed out in the previous chapter, your mindset is a critical element to success. The way you perceive things can be the asset that propels you forward towards your dreams. Additionally, your perception can be the liability that propels you backward.

Whatever type of investment you choose from the subsequent pages, you are bound to encounter hard times. You will tread through rocky roads that can crimp the fire of passion in your stomach. I am not suggesting that your money will melt into thin air or fail to yield profits. That's not it. My point is that I have run into financial distress while trying to save for the future and spend at the moment.

Everyone goes through life deciding whether to spend now on something you really want or sacrifice for a greater goal and invest. I recognize that it can seem very hard and, in a few situations, impossible.

Your family, friends, and associates might think you are going insane. They might not agree with your decision to invest while your current needs continue to pile-up. At times like these, your only solace lies deep in your spirit. It lies in your mindset. You can do anything you put your mind to as long as you work hard, give it your all, and don't listen to what anyone else has to say. It's your world, you can do what you want. If you want to make sacrifices now to achieve your goal of life long financial freedom, this book is for you.

To adjust your mindset for long-term wealth, you must learn to do several things. There is a long queue of them, and I will unveil them in the next few sections.

The funny thing about change is that it can be so subtle you don't even recognize it. After months and years go by, you will notice the sensational change in yourself, your finances, and your lifestyle. There is too much to discuss. We'd better get started.

Questions Investors Have to Ask Themselves

- **Risk-taking**

Risk-taking refers to your ability to take an educated shot in the dark. In our case, it is the habit of plunging your best efforts into something that has little certainty. If you desire to own a duplex in Scarsdale or Cherry Hills Village, you may save up your funds and achieve your dreams in three years. However, if you have chosen to grow your wealth by investing in stocks, securities, and so on, you will be faced with an entirely different situation. You will use up a chunk of your salary. Cut back on expenses. These are things people don't want to hear or do. You will be unable to be certain whether you will live long enough to reap the benefits from your efforts. You also stand a chance of losing short-term if something goes wrong in the market. All the while, you could have bought a new car and flash your financial spending without regard. Knowing all of these obstacles and still choosing to invest makes you sound like a crackbrain to people who don't understand the benefits an investing lifestyle offers.

Nevertheless, taking risks is the number one habit of every successful entrepreneur. It is the habit of investors alike. Nothing is entirely sure, and it is incredibly hard to place your life savings into a dream that has no absolute guarantee.

Have you ever staked a full month's salary in a casino? Let's assume you were not drunk. Would you do it in your right mind? I guess not. But the wild spirit to do something like that is the exact spirit to make it big in the world of investments. The difference between putting your money in the hands of a casino versus putting your money in the hands of the stock market is simple. The odds are stacked in your favor when properly investing in the market. Hence, you are now the casino with favorable odds. The odds are stacked in your favor with these seven investments.

Staking your life-saving at a casino is not what I am about to recommend. I only want you to understand that you'd need a similar spirit of firmness and strict resolution. This adamant spirit will help you keep staking and investing when it looks like you should have returned home and spent your money. Casino gambling is a loser's game. Investing is a winner's game.

- **Making money**

"If you would be wealthy, think of saving as well as getting."

— BENJAMIN FRANKLIN

Making money is the most vital step before investing money. Before you even dream about investing, you must have funds or monthly income you can invest with. You cannot possibly invest what you do not have. You will need to make enough for now and the future. So, making money is a necessary foundation for long-term wealth building.

Undeniably, money is not a commodity that the average person can have enough of. We make efforts to acquire money day in, day out, and there is no stopping, no matter how much we receive. Nevertheless, there are differences between a person who can afford a 2021 Mercedes and someone who has nothing to eat the next morning. This does not convey that you should be wealthy enough to afford a Mercedes before considering investments. It is just that you will likely have enough to put away towards investments if you have enough to purchase a car without completely emptying your wallet.

Am I suggesting that you cannot invest in the future if you are struggling to feed yourself?

Yes.

You cannot save or invest if you are struggling to eat.

Nobody saves when their budget only allows them to pay for food and rent. You can begin to save only when food is no longer a part of your basic expenses. You should also have enough to take care of your immediate and basic needs. You need not live a flashy lifestyle or cruise the streets in expensive cars. The moment you have enough to cover unanticipated expenses or open a savings account, you are fit to set up an investment portfolio.

Whatever stage you find yourself in, you are going to need more money as soon as you begin to invest. You will no longer have as much as you used to have in your possession. You will also need to strike a balance between your immediate demands and your urgent future decisions.

The only way you can meet this demand is to make more money. You need to broaden your mind on your current profession, as well as the existing skills you have. There has to be a way to enlarge your income. Take a deep pause and think it through. You need more money!

- **Managing money**

Have you thought about how you can make more money?

Pretty good! Let's open the next part that borders along that; the surefire way to manage money. Managing money is a whole different ball game. It is about the art and science of using money most judiciously. It is about the antics of earning more than a million each year, and not ending up with a few thousand at the end. It is a verifiable fact that people tend to have broader needs as they earn more. They find more things they should have, more people they should help, and sometimes, more people they should impress. It should not surprise you that you notice something similar about yourself.

"The real art is not in making money; it is in keeping it."

— PROVERB

It is hard to make money and it is easy to spend it. By any means, you have to guarantee that your expenses are pretty much within your grip. Your expenses should never grow bigger as your income gets bigger, within reason, of course.

This may sound tricky and difficult. In particular, because it happens in the form of a habit. You only notice that your heart clings to something. The second your bank account is healthy, you splurge a little. At that same time, the utility company is withdrawing its dues. The dealership has its share. The banks are extracting their transaction charge, and so on. In the end, you are left with little, and you still have a list of things to buy. Entirely true, isn't it? I told you I have been in these shoes before!

Now, this circle seems natural and unbreakable. It seems so certain that there is no surefire way to alter it and expand the money you have. Can this cycle ever be reformed? Yes, and you don't have to rack your brain for how to accomplish this. All you have to do is abide by the following steps.

Track Spending Habits by Using a Scale of Preference

Similar to my first recommendation, making a scale of preference is a safe course for managing your money. You might agree with my first point. You might say, "yeah, I have to cut down on my personal consumption." But your big problem will kindle when you are not sure what to trim off your budget. You keep wondering what to cut first and what not to cut. Soon your life spirals into an entirely new planet of indecision.

Just like the first situation, this is not out of this world. It is something that happens all the time. An average person runs into a decision-making dilemma, and they often end up making the wrong choice. The only way you can solve this problem is to create a scale of preference.

What is the scale of preference? It is a simple document that highlights your needs according to their level of importance. Complicated? No. It is a simple list. It could be drafted with a classroom pen, computer, sticky notepads, anything. It contains everything you intend to buy alongside their prices. It is, however, structured in a way that the essential item is ranked first on the list, regardless of the cost. Most important at the top, least important at the bottom.

This means that if you need gum and a toothbrush, you might want to rank that toothbrush first. A toothbrush has more to do with your health than chewing gum. There are no special rules to arrange items on this table. All you need to do is take a brief moment and reflect on your needs. Add your wants too. List out the things you want and those you need, then begin to list them on your scale of preference, each according to its level of importance. No one is suing you for financial misappropriation if you do not follow this scale of preference in your purchasing decisions. Despite that, if you have taken all that time to create the list, you are intent on managing your finances and more willing to follow it. If you want positive change, it might be ideal to follow the scale of preference.

- **Avoid consumer debt**

Let's get off the ground by answering the sole question; what does consumer debt mean? Consumer debts are debts you rack up on goods and services that do not appreciate in value. You are either purchasing them, so you could be the last person to use them, or you would be selling them off at giveaway prices if you ever consider selling them. Would you be able to recognize these goods around your house? Shoes, Clothes, Cars (by now, I bet you can see that I love cars) and similar assets.

Most of these items are accessories. They do not typically add to your financial worth. They often depreciate in the long run and become less valuable. Most of them are not vital to your life, happiness, and achievement as a human being. Yet, Investopedia reports that an average human spends up to 90% of their expenses on consumer goods. It gets more interesting when you remember that the most expensive of these goods are purchased on credit. Consumer debt also comes with higher interest rates than most other types of debt.

"There are more consumer debts than any other kind of debt in the world."

— JULIA KAGAN

Where does this leave you? If you are in debt, it is likely because you have spent too much on consumer goods. Your consumer goods are where most, if not all, your funds are going. It is time you check your spending habits and choose between what is necessary and what you really should avoid. Start paying extra attention to your credit card, dealership, utility, and such debts that you incur from consumer goods. Make it a priority to monitor where your money is going. You will be pleasantly surprised by the amount of money you can save.

- **Not losing money**

Have you ever heard Warren Buffet's first rule of wealth?

It says, "Never lose money." It gets interesting when you learn that the second rule says, "You should never forget rule 1."

It seems entirely sane to advise you not to lose money. Isn't it? Now that I think of it, I wonder if anyone would ever advise you to lose money. Everyone would tell you not to lose money, and who would forget that anyway?

Simple as it sounds, the "never lose money" rule is one of the golden rules you can hold onto in personal finance. You might spend a few dollars at the nearest coffee shop because you enjoy the coffee. In addition, the conversations you have with the same employee at the same time everyday is enjoyable. What's wrong with that? Nothing at all. Then how on earth is it possible to not lose money!?

Now I am sure you will start to wonder what Warren Buffet had in his head when he profoundly uttered that statement. But it is pretty simple. No matter what you do with your money, you must guarantee that you profit or add value to your life. Think of one item you consistently spend money on. If this item adds little or nothing to your value or wealth, you will be losing money if you continue this spending habit.

As his natural philosophy, Warren Buffet would never invest in businesses that seem too complicated to understand. His records proved that he could be one of INTEL's owners today, but he declined to invest because he was unsure how it operated. Instead, he invested a lot of his money into the chewing gum industry. No regrets; to be successful, you don't need to invest in every opportunity that comes your way. If you like what you hear and the profit margins make sense in your brain, that's the investment you should go with. Not only an investment that looks good but an investment that you can easily understand. Buffett invested in what he was sure about, and you can attest to the result of his investments.

- **Keep an eye out**

Fairness does not exist in the functioning of humanity. Humans are distinctively creative. We all see things differently, and it is super hard, if not impossible, to align your goals with the goals of someone else. In a business situation where men gather from here and there, each with their distinctive interests, it is impossible to be treated fairly. Even when there are clear rules and regulations, people will always long for a way to bypass these rules and cheat others.

What does this mean to you? You should never expect to be treated fairly. Have a proactive mindset rather than a reactive mindset. Go out there in the world and take what you want, don't wait for things to just roll your way because some of the greatest things in life won't come to you. The greatest things in life are the creations you build yourself.

Investing is not a solo game. You are going to deal with humans and resources. Most of these humans have the same zeal as you. They are looking to up their profit and maintain their wealth for the rest of their lives. Some are way beyond that; however, they are bound to be greedy, dissatisfied, selfish, and sly. Just as the rule applies in politics, there are no permanent friends in business either.

I had a long time friend with whom I shared many great memories with. As children we went on family vacations, buddied up for Boy Scout retreats, his father even coached our little league baseball team. Recently he was in need of an automobile, so I tried to find him a good car for an affordable price. I found him a dependable car but the brakes were long past due. Being from a mechanical family, I fixed the brakes, replaced the air filter, and changed the oil. He wasn't under the impression that I would work on "his car" and was offended that I would do so without his permission. Long story short, both of our feelings got hurt in the process. Due to a business transaction that left both of us in a misunderstanding, we no longer communicate. Be selective and careful whom you do business with. Doing a favor, and doing a business deal are different principles. Be sure you establish which one it is before you get mixed up with a friend. Be perceptive enough to foresee things. Always try to visualize where things could end up before it's too late.

Let's consider another real-life situation. Mike Shaw, a real estate baron living in the United Kingdom, heard about some hot real estate in Highland Park, Texas, so he flew in to check out the property. When arriving on-site, he was content by the size and value of the asset, so he decided to pay immediately. There were no official documents, and Mike didn't mind because the seller was a reliable old friend. Surprisingly, the seller swindled him. He had sold to someone else, and disappeared almost immediately with all of Mike's money. Mike Shaw had just lost his life savings because he assumed he was dealing with a trusted friend from his past.

The lesson to you?

Trust people, just not blindly. Do not skip vital procedures because things seem "all good" to you. It is a piece of candid advice. You will need it moving forward.

- **Diversify**

Diversification is the art of expanding your income streams and investments. It is healthy to have more than once source of income, and similarly, more than one kind of investment. The benefits of diversifying your portfolio is precisely why I insist that you consider more than one investment type in the following chapters.

If you diversify, you will achieve mastery status over the market. One of the benefits is avoiding surprises. As long as you have enough diversity between your investments, the rewards from one source can immensely compensate whatever gets lost in another sector.

Some so-called "experts" will tell you diversification is not necessary because they know of this one stock that will shoot your portfolio up 1000%. How do they know a stock will shoot up 1000%? They don't. Yeah, I have heard of people winning the lottery or hitting the jackpot at a casino too. For long-term investing, diversification is encouraged because, in thirty years, the marketplace will look vastly different than it looks today. Caveat emptor (buyer beware). Proceed with caution when approached with a get-rich-quick scheme. If it were true, they wouldn't be trying so hard to sell you on it.

Another point. You can take care of surprises by diversifying your investments. If one of your investment's goes down significantly, you can expect better yields in another sector, as long as you are giving all your investments a similar opportunity to grow.

• Education

Now that you have chosen to become an investor, your education must begin in earnest. You may have a degree or a higher certificate from college, but financial literacy is a different crux in entirety. Not only do you have to train yourself in it, but you must also understand that it is much more important in the game of life than the formal schooling you have had.

"Formal education will make you a living. Self-education will make you a fortune."

— JIM ROHM

Your knowledge should not only end in general financial education. You'd have to learn about a niche you wish to pursue (stocks, real estate, baseball cards, et cetera). You have to understand your investments. You want to have an idea of what you are funneling your money into, how it has previously operated, and how it will possibly operate in the future. You should apply Warren Buffet's rule of never investing in something you have little knowledge about. And remember, as Benjamin Franklin professes, an investment in knowledge pays the best interest back to you.

- **Ignore the others**

This is the final point. It would be entirely unfair to wrap this chapter up without talking about it. When you have a certain amount of wealth, you will likely cruise the world with people who maintain a similar status. Some of them may be wealthier than you, and some may not be as wealthy as you. These peers will form your circle of friendship. You will likely have some friends from primary school and others from college, work, et cetera. Relationships are one of man's most cherished possessions. Many of your friends will lavishly spend money. They might expect you to live the same way. A saying that will stand until the end of time is very relevant in this case. *Stop trying to keep up with the Jones's.* You will fail if you try.

ENDING THOUGHTS

It is once again, your responsibility to reach your goals. You have big dreams, and you are gunning for it. You have your life, your thoughts, and your perspectives on personal finance. You are entirely different from anyone else. As such, you are not going to be a part of the old lifestyle anymore.

I have to reiterate that this will be one of your biggest challenges. Your parents, spouse, kids, colleagues, and friends, will pressure you. Hopefully, your family may get the hang of what you are doing and try not to bother you. But you have made your choice, regardless of the world's views, and you are going to stand by it! Firm decision making does not come easy for everyone but it is essential in a world full of distractions.

Lions don't listen to the opinions of sheep.

Are you able to recognize your life's dream deep down inside yourself and picture it vividly?

Are you able to adopt a positive frame of mind that will propel you forward into the world of success?

You are all set to see the most promising investments in the world for building long-term wealth. And I am going to uncover them for you, one after the other.

Flip the page, let's get started.

PART II
7 INVESTMENTS THAT MEET THE TEST OF TIME

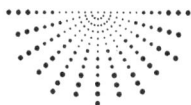

3

DIVIDEND PAYING STOCKS AND COMPOUND INTEREST

At this stage, you clearly understand your life's ambitions and dreams. You also understand the mindset you should have and what you should do away with if you are going to be wealthy throughout your lifetime. Your mind is your biggest asset.

All through the next few pages, you and I will put our heads together and discuss various things on stocks, shares, and digital currency. I bet these will be topics you have heard about, and you think you have some idea what they mean.

However, I promise we are going to touch areas that you have most likely not heard before. We may also uncover facts that conflict with a lot of assumptions you have previously held. I fear that you may lose out if you begin to relate these facts with the rumors you have picked up on the street.

As such, I strongly recommend that you let your predispositions slip off your mind. If you have never done self-educating research about the stock market, that's okay too.

> *"The illiterate of the 21st century will not be those who cannot read and write, but those who cannot learn, unlearn, and relearn."*
>
> — ALVIN TOFFLER

The general population of young adults could care less about investing. You are already ahead of the curve by choosing to read this book. It's no wonder why young adults don't care about investing their money and growing it. Investors in corporate suits make investing seem boring, numbing, and mindless. The culture of investing is outdated. No 20-year-old wants to sit in a classroom all afternoon learning from a 65-year-old retiree preaching about what a 401(K) is. It makes sense why investing is not a popular topic among young adults. That is something I want to change with this book. I want a 15-year-old to be as engaged as that 65-year-old retiree because building wealth is interesting. It all depends on your frame of mind whether you take fondly to a subject or you leave it by the wayside.

Hopefully, learning about the stock market from someone similar in age will strike your curiosity and ambitious behavior. Without further ado, let's begin.

The Stock Market

The Stock Market is the meeting point where buyers and sellers meet. It refers to the virtual or physical location where you get into talks with people who are interested in trading stock, bonds, and so forth. In the United States, the most popular stock exchange markets are the New York Stock Exchange and the American Stock Exchange. Nasdaq, jointly owned by the United States and Canada, is a prominent one too.

You may wonder, what does stock even mean?

Simply put, stock refers to the ownership of a company. A company sells a percentage of ownership to generate funds for the business. Sometimes, a company faces financial challenges. To grow, a company releases its stock publicly to raise funds. The most common way a company generates funds are from banks, but even banks run into this financial imbroglio. Besides, some companies require a lot more than an average commercial bank can lend. What is their solution? Trading stock.

One of the ways a company could raise funds is to sell its stock in the marketplace at a cost per share. It means that they will be selling a percentage of ownership to anyone who has the funds to boost their business. The ownership is broken into fragments referred to as stock. If you own a considerable amount of stock, you might soon become a primary decision-maker in a company. Company stock is set up through an initial public offering.

The company releases a set of shares in a primary market. It gives members of the public the option to purchase a percentage of ownership. In turn, they financially contribute to their faithful investors. A group of shares is called stock. These shares are not complete ownership of a company; the total released shares may range between 5% to 30% of the company's worth. They are set up in a primary market and sold in a secondary market.

Stocks or shares are sold in a secondary market by brokers and bought by buyers like you and I. Alternatively, anyone who has held the shares of a company for some time may decide to sell. You retain every right on that stock the instant you buy it. By default, the company is not directly involved in the purchase or sale of their shares. Their shares are sold, their funds are raised, and that is all that matters.

The stock market is one of the biggest and most productive markets to invest your funds. It is the perfect "bank" for all persons who have money they'd like to put away. It is way more productive than reserving your funds in banks. If you have ever wondered what banks do with your money besides loaning it to other people for mortgages and business loans, they also invest your money into the market. A hidden fact is that banks themselves engage in stock trades with the funds gathered from people who decide to save with them. Banks generate a huge gain from the market by investing your money and pay you a minimal token, aka you're too small to see the periodic interest. By directly engaging in the stock market, you are eliminating third parties like banks, and attaining all the profit for yourself.

If you decide to put this book down at any point, I would suggest doing it at the end of a paragraph and mark it. The following pages will transition into a block system. When you eventually transition into investing in the market, use these seven investments as an abridged version.

At this stage, you have a clear idea about what stocks are. It is time to answer a burning question.

***Why should a person aspiring for long-term
wealth invest in the stock market?***

- **Stocks are easy to purchase**

There is always stock on the market for anyone who has the funds. That makes it easier than other types of investments. You may be specific about the company whose stock you are buying. You might simply buy the most promising stocks you find on the market, too, regardless of the company. You can always get your stocks online, as long as your account is set up and active. Alternatively, you might buy through a financial advisor or broker.

- **Effortless to sell (liquidity)**

Do you have a reason to dispense your stock? You can do it this minute. That is how easy stocks can change hands in the stock market. While it may not sound like a great idea, selling your shares is an option you can always consider. For definite reasons, you may choose to sell a particular stock and purchase another. There are always buyers around, whether the trend is bullish or bearish. The only snag is that you might sell at a loss. Still, you will always have enough to take on another stock. Alternatively, if you are investing in a company you founded, it will be more difficult to pull out your funds.

- **Shares make you a company owner**

Another advantage of being a shareholder is that you are equally a company owner. It is pretty clear that you own only a fraction, and that might get bigger with time. Even if it doesn't get bigger, the prospect of being one of the owners in a big company is attractive. People want to know that after working hard for some corporations, there is a corporation somewhere that sincerely belongs to them. They may not be in charge of its operations, but their funds keep it going. Its success means their success, and it has a duty to remit funds and updates to them. I enjoy this canny style of owing companies.

- **Entrepreneurs take risks**

Engaging in stocks is a unique method of becoming an entrepreneur. You may not notice it, but you exhibit every feature of an entrepreneur when you deal in stocks. You'll have to take risks, invest your time in research, and try to make a killing in the stock market.

- **Magic of compounding**

This is the most important reason you should ever consider the stock market. Compound interest is arguably the eighth wonder of the world. Your funds do not add up in ones and twos. They compound. Investing in the stock market is the only way a thousand dollars can become a million dollars without you touching a single thing. You do not have to call anyone or do anything; your money keeps multiplying. As a smart entrepreneur investing in your future, this sounds like the perfect thing for you. You should picture what you stand to gain if you invest a big chunk of your earnings. So far, stocks still offer some of the best returns. For someone in their 20's, compound interest is your shortcut to building wealth.

Having unveiled the reasons why you should

consider investing in stocks, we will proceed
with an important question.

What Type of Stocks Should You Venture Into?

No questions about it, venturing into stocks is pretty simple. But it isn't going to be as straightforward as creating an account and selecting a stock. You know that, don't you? There are different companies in the stock market. Some are fast-growing, international, multimillion-dollar worth, and others are worth billions or trillions of dollars. There are various ways of classifying all these companies. They also do not place the same value on their stocks. This is all to say that there is a lot to know about the stock market. There are different kinds of stocks on the market, and a brilliant investor has to learn the ropes before opening their wallet. Do you remember what we said about sparing your time to educate yourself? Good.

Two Types of Stocks on the Market

- **Common stocks**

Common Stocks are stocks that offer voting rights to their owners. They are the type of stocks you buy when you are aiming to become one of the owners of a corporation. You want the right to vote when the company makes crucial decisions such as the selection of board directors. You also want to be an essential part of the company. Typically, you'd have one vote with one share.

So, buying a lot of shares will increase your pull in the decision-making process. In some cases, common stocks offer dividends. But dividends are determined by the financial situation of the company. The company would worry about fulfilling its financial obligations to companies, bondholders, and creditors outside the company, before you.

This is exactly why the company will make clearing its external debts their priority if the company ever declares bankruptcy. By implication, you and other common stockholders may never make a profit. There is some chance that you will lose money here, and that means going against Warren Buffet's very first law of investment. Do you remember what it says?

Common stocks are arguably not the best choice for anyone looking to build long-term wealth. We will agree that if the company hits the jackpot, you might make a whole lot of money by selling some of your stock, which would have a much higher value. You also stand a chance of becoming a top man in a big corporation. But what if it fails? You should remember that financial compensation is not the priority in this type of stock.

All of these point to one thing; this may not be the best choice for someone looking to build long-term wealth with tactical calculations. Your big aspiration should have nothing to do with voting or not. Instead, you should be obsessed with how to generate your wealth and to maintain it for as long as you live. Though some common stocks are promising, and you should not rule them out in entirety, it should not be your priority.

- **Preferred stocks**

Preferred Stocks are really our preferred stocks. They are stocks that are usually explicitly issued to investors. They sometimes offer some amount of ownership, especially if you are purchasing a lot of them. But that is not the priority. Ownership is as nonobligatory as a dividend in the previous type of stocks. If you manage a stock like this, you can always sell it off when there is high demand. Preferred stocks guarantee that you will be funded if the company goes bankrupt. The best of all, you receive repetitive dividend payments every quarter. This is the point where I am sure you must be wondering...

What's a Dividend?

Dividend refers to the compensation given by a company to its investors. It is a form of payment that the company issues out to investors in reward for their loyal support. It is usually generated from the profits made by the company after any debt has been cleared. Dividends may not come in if the company is battling financial perplexity. With that said, a dividend yield is typically stable. In a situation where a company is battling financial perplexity, they will notify shareholders of a change in dividend payment for the upcoming quarter. Dividends may be paid in cash, additional shares, or some other agreed means. Usually, the board of directors in a company decide on the dividend. Depending on the class of the company you invest in, your dividends may be high or low. This is why you need to know the classification of companies on the stock market.

The Classification of Companies on the Stock Market

- **Classification by location**

Companies are sometimes classified according to their location. Many stocks are traded on the US markets, yet they have no establishment in the US at all. Many others are established in the United States, they are involved in international transactions. The expansion potential of these companies may determine their profitability. But this is not a prominent factor to consider when selecting your stock. There are three more types of classification.

- **Classification by company size**

Companies are also classified according to their sizes. There are three classifications in this category; the large-cap, mid-size cap, and small-cap. Recognizing cap size will give you more intuition when evaluating stocks you'd like to purchase. Large-cap companies are companies that have a market value of 10 billion dollars or more. Stability is the most guaranteed feature of large-cap companies. Their stock value is usually low. As such, you'd have to invest an enormous amount if you are looking for a sizable return. However, they are established and would have no trouble paying dividends, which a smart investor would reinvest and let compound interest perform its magic. Mid-size companies have a market value between $2 to $10 billion, and small caps are valued between 300 million to $2 billion. These are growing companies too. Small-cap companies have a higher risk because they are less established. With more volatility, small caps can massively increase in stock price or devastatingly fall. Investing in revolutionary small-cap companies have enormous potential in the long run. Amazon and Netflix were small-cap companies years ago. Investing early with the intuition that a small-cap company will become a large-cap stock some day has immeasurable positive upside.

- **Classification by industry**

Markets are classified according to their industry too. As an illustration, you may engage in technology, education, and so on. The sector can determine the prospect of the company's success. It can determine how fierce a company competes, expectations of company performance, and profitability. For example, the fossil fuel sector might not be a good investment in 2020 because the world is shifting its efforts toward clean and renewable energy.

- **Classification by style**

Lastly, growth and value stocks are variations in the business world. Growth stocks refer to the stock of companies that are established or have the potential to become established in the near future. These companies are already set up. However, they are looking to expand; they would require support from investors to achieve their highest potential. Investing in such funds can guarantee higher stakes in the long run. But it certainly comes with little or no dividends. Cisco, Oracle, and Sun Microsystems are firsthand examples of such companies in the United States. Value stocks are typically undervalued stocks. With the proper business moves made by a prosperous company quarter after quarter, value stocks can soar to new heights. These types of stocks are especially risky but have the capability to produce quick returns.

From all of these, it is glaring that you have to be methodical about your investments. You do not wake up and simply venture into the world of market trading. You need to consider many statistics.

Preparation and execution are equally important. What you may learn today may be something contradictory to what you learn tomorrow. The important thing is that we do not stay complacent in our ability to learn, unlearn, and relearn

Dividend stocks and compounded interest go hand in hand. High dividend paying stocks have the capability to create explosive gains in a young person's portfolio over time. A young person's greatest asset is their time.

High Dividend Paying Stocks

As Arielle O' shea, a financial reporter explains, high dividend-paying stocks are the best stocks for investors. Dividend stocks pay a yield on the shares you own. Also known as income stocks, high dividend-paying stocks have been the most rewarding type of stocks in the past forty years. They are usually paid quarterly, and they offer guaranteed returns on investment. Since you are trying to avoid risks as much as you can, this is going to be one of your best bets. Especially if you are young and looking to grow your wealth long-term. Young investors often choose high dividend-paying stocks over any other type of investment. The value of the dividend is measured by a yield, which is usually calculated in percentages.

- **Calculating a dividend yield**

Pick a company listed on the stock market. Use the formula below:

Annual Dividend per share *divided by* Stock Price per share *equals* Dividend Yield

Let's take Johnson and Johnson (JNJ) as an example. JNJ is a great company that pays great dividends. They currently pay an annual dividend of ($4.04) per share. We take the annual dividend of ($4.04), divide it by the current stock price of ($149.35), and you get your dividend yield of (2.71%).

Annual Dividend / Stock Price = Dividend Yield

$4.04 / $149.35 = 2.71%

This formula to calculate your dividend yield shows that JNJ stock has a yield of 2.71%. An ideal high dividend paying stock should have a steady return above 1.95%. As the stock price changes, so does the dividend yield.

Additionally, Companies can increase or decrease their dividends at any time.

Currently, the Top 13 Highest Dividend Paying Stocks in the World (based off of dividend yield) are:

Company	Dividend($)	Dividend Yield(%)
(NHI) National Health Investors Inc.	1.1	7.36
(BNS) The Bank Of Nova Scotia	0.9	6.29
(BCE) BCE Inc.	0.83	5.76
(CVX) Chevron Corp.	1.29	5.69
(BMO) Bank of Montreal	1.06	5.59
(TRP) TC Energy Corp.	0.81	5.46
(PFG) Principal Financial Group Inc.	0.56	5.31
(TD) The Toronto-Dominion Bank	0.79	5.13
(STX) Seagate Technology Plc.	0.65	5.0
(OMC) Omnicom Group Inc.	0.65	4.88
(RY) Royal Bank of Canada	1.08	4.67
(DUK) Duke Energy Corp.	0.95	4.60
(ALE) Allete Inc.	0.62	4.53
(NKSH) National Bankshares Inc.	0.67	4.49

(accurate numbers as of July 2020)

Use this list as your benchmark of the top dividend paying stocks. To clarify, there are other stocks that pay higher dividends but they are usually penny stocks that a long-term investor wouldn't hold in their portfolio. Picking the highest paying dividend stocks is not a simple solution to a complex problem of selecting the right stocks for your portfolio. When calculating our example dividend yield, I used the company, Johnson and Johnson, as an example. Johnson and Johnson's dividend yield is 2.71%. Compared to the top 13 highest dividend paying stocks, Johnson and Johnson's dividend yield looks significantly smaller, but that should not detour you from choosing JNJ or a company with a modest dividend yield.

If I had to give you the most crucial trick successful investors use when picking stocks, it would be:

Don't make your investment decisions based off a single statistic, good or bad.

A stock's dividend yield does not fully encapsulate the

performance or profit you will receive. Personally, I believe Johnson and Johnson is a better stock option than some of the highest dividend-yielding companies listed above. The *dividends* a company gives you is as significant as *earnings growth, stability, management, price-earnings ratio,* and *relative strength.*

In Chapter 10, we will discuss a step by step process on how you can set up your individualized investment portfolio. After you read and review the content in each chapter, you will be ready for Chapter 10, Crafting an Exceptional Portfolio. Until then, we will continue to dive into these seven investments.

Five Reasons You Should Consider High Dividend Paying Stocks

- **Guaranteed return on investment over time**

As a chap who puts his head down working hard day and night, you deserve some reassurance. You have chosen to save and invest in the future while others are living lavish lives. You deserve to know that all your effort is not going to vanish without something substantial to show for it. High paying dividend stocks offer assurance. Dividend stocks yield a higher return over time because these stocks give you free money every quarter. The longer you leave your money in a dividend paying stock, the more interest you will accrue. Your finances will not go missing if the company runs into difficulty, unlike common shares. Besides, if you are tactical about selecting your stocks, the companies you are invested in will not have to sour in stock price. Of course, you would like the company's stock price to rise, but the effects of compound interest are more powerful over time than the current stock price.

- **Minimal risks**

The presence of low risk is a reason you should consider dividend stocks. A company that pays a high dividend is established. The company is no longer focused on expanding or generating huge profits. As such, a large share of their profits are distributed to their investors. What this means is that the company considers investors first. Also, they are well off and can conveniently refund investors like you, even when they go bankrupt. That shows that a lot of risk is removed from your investment. Anyone looking to build steady long-term wealth would love to consider an investment category like this.

- **Offers assurances in volatile markets**

Even when the market is continuously drifting into unpredictability, high dividend-paying stocks are your best choice. As I have earlier mentioned, they are well off. They can weather economic downturns without a fuss. Selecting preferred stocks also mean that the company considers paying you a necessity. If the company has a good track record of profit-making, feel comfortable risking your capital in their company with little to lose.

- **Yield**

This is the sole reason you are stepping into the market at all. You want your funds to yield overtime and multiply itself. You want to go into the market with a thousand dollars and return with thousands of dollars. With high dividend-paying stocks, there are no ifs or buts. You will achieve just that with your funds. Reinvesting your profits for a span of twenty years in high dividend paying stocks is one of the easiest and full proof ways to achieve *millionaire status*.

- **Two sources of income**

Did you notice the double avenue that high paying dividends open up to you? First, you earn when the company releases dividends. You also receive compounded dividends after the first dividend payment. If you have chosen to reserve your funds for a long time, your dividends will be increased and expanded by your annual returns with compound interest. If you have invested $1000, for instance, your yearly yield might be 5%. Then you have $1,050 as the next year's investment and that's for doing nothing at all. The following year, your $1,050 compounds again at 5%. Not to mention, stock prices tend to go up through the year. So there is no telling what your initial $1,000 will be worth. Definitely a lot more than $1,050.

I f you close this book and take a second to think things through, you will realize that dividend-paying stocks *multiplied by* compounded interest is indeed the eighth wonder of the world. Growing your wealth is much more significant than parading as a company board member when it has no guarantees. Look for ways to generate high paying dividends, and you can see that your old dreams are becoming feasible again.

How Can You Secure High Dividend-Paying Stocks?

Securing good dividend stocks is easy. It involves just a few steps and targets. However, you will have to pay attention to the tips and tricks below before venturing into any of them. Often, people fall into a ditch when they try to skip or trivialize some of these steps. So, I strongly recommend that you do not skip any of them.

- **Look for long-term profitability**

The first step is to keep your eye on companies that have recorded steady profits. You want to be sure that the company has steadily recorded profits in the last four to five years. You do not need them to document an exceedingly high-profit margin, such as a 30-70% increase. Anything between a steady 7-30% increase is proof that the company has long-term profitability. The location of the company should not be a factor.

- **Check their dividend records**

The instant your preferred company has an established profitability record, the next factor to consider is its dividend paying record. As a financial advisor, Andrew Bloomenthal suggests, it is crucial to confirm the company's dividend-paying rates in previous years. You want to be entirely sure that the company declares high dividends, but it also pays dividends each year or quarterly, and it records a steady yield. Companies will change their dividends whenever they deem it fit. A company usually increases or decreases its dividend at the end of a quarter.

- **Steer clear of firms with a debt-to-equality ratio that exceeds 2.00**

I strongly recommend avoiding firms with extremely high debt to equality ratio. You might receive a little dividend or yield if the company has a debt ratio of this rate. Even when profit is made, the company would be concerned about paying these debts before releasing dividends. As such, declared bonuses might be unrealistic. With a high debt ratio, there is no telling when the company will temporarily or indefinitely suspend dividend payments. Any news that the company will no longer be paying dividends, the hype and attention that draws will most likely drop the share price of the stock immediately and consistently over the near future.

- **Research the industry trend**

Most of the time, the company's sector influences the profitability of the stock. You should make defensive stocks your target. They are stocks of companies that produce goods and services that are used in the house. Considering the high rise in demand for computers as an example, a computer manufacturing company might stand a high chance of profit rather than a company that produces ammunition during peace time. If the birth rate rises steeply, there is a chance that a company providing baby products might make higher profits over the coming years. There are no guarantees that your company will be the leader in that industry. However, there are chances that your company might do just fine. Timing the market according to industry trends is not the goal, but a skill worth mentioning.

Action to Take: Buy Dividend Paying Stocks

Highly Respectable Dividend Stocks Include:

1. Procter & Gamble (NYSE: **PG**)
2. IBM (NYSE: **IBM**)
3. Walmart (NYSE: **WMT**)
4. Coca-Cola (NYSE: **KO**)
5. Walgreens Boots Alliance (Nasdaq: **WBA**)

All five companies have paid and raised their dividends for the past 25 consecutive years.

ENDING THOUGHTS

In this chapter, we discovered the overwhelming benefits of dividend paying stocks. It is a no brainer that dividend stocks are one of the best investments ever for a young investor. I personally know parents who set up an investment account specifically for dividend stocks so their newly born child can add 20 years of compound interest to their name before their 20th birthday. These accounts generate massive income to pay for college, life's pleasures, or security in a prosperous future.

Allow dividend paying stocks and compound interest be

your best friend as you age. If we invest in our 20's, by the time we get our first grey hair we can celebrate the life long achievement we have made in guaranteeing a bright future.

Tell me again, are you sure you do not want to storm into the bank right now, grab your savings out of there, and take a crack at high dividend-paying stocks?

Cheers!

4

S&P 500 INDEX FUND

For a few pages in the last chapter, we talked about the size of companies. I specifically mentioned when researching stocks, they can be assessed according to the size of the companies involved. This is why we have the large-cap companies, mid-size cap, and the small caps. I said large-cap companies are companies that have a bucket value of 10 billion dollars and beyond. To be specific, we will say 10-200 billion dollars.

I also pointed out that mid-cap companies have a market value between 2 to 10 billion dollars, and small caps are valued between 300 million to 2 billion dollars. Do you remember all of these? Awesome! You will have a good idea of what I am about to discuss.

S&P 500 Index is one of the various means of investing in the stock market. It is a form of index investment, and it is a cap-weighted investment.

Don't fret.

I will explain every bit of this, and I will begin by clarifying the terms. I have to make it clear that this is technical.

Though, I will keep it short and discuss the basic principles you need to know. We will discuss the essentials of S&P index funds, and why you should consider investing in it. Let's get started.

Index Funds

"Index mutual fund is an easy, hands-off, diversified, low-cost way to invest in the stock market."

— DAYANA YOCHIM

It is a unique form of investment that concentrates on a few groups of stocks. It pays attention to the selected groups and provides a rundown of their performance in the market. Index funds issue their risks, returns, and prospects to the general public. Usually, an index is handled by a company, a brokerage, or an investment bank. There are several of them in the United States.

An index fund is a form of investment where investors choose to buy a portion of the market rather than one company's stock. For example, an index may cover the top 5 companies in a sector. If you select such an index, you are directly investing in these stocks without having to choose one yourself. This way, if the sector's profitability increases, your investment will too.

The index company entirely decides the procedure for selecting a multitude of individual company stocks. The significant advantage of index investments is that they offer a lower risk than all other types of investments, and it offers access to select companies that would otherwise be too expensive. It also comes with a flatter management expense compared to paying a professional to pick and manage each of your stocks. There are several index funds available to purchase on the stock market, but the most extensive index in the United States is the S&P 500 Index.

A peculiar advantage of index funds is that they offer you the opportunity to invest in tens or hundreds of companies at the same time at an affordable rate. If the index is adopting the common stock pattern like Nasdaq-100, it would mean that you own a stake in all of those companies. If the index fund chooses the dividend-yielding model, you will have investments in companies that would most likely produce impressive yield results all through your investment years.

Let's Get Into the Essentials, What Does S&P 500 Index Encompass?

S&P (In full, *Standard and Poor*) 500 is the most extensive stock in the United States. According to Ken Clark, an investment analyst, S&P 500 stocks cover up to $28.1 trillion of the US Stock Market as of March 2020. This means that the S&P 500 alone covers up to 75% of the United States Equity Market. It is strong enough to be considered a benchmark for investors.

S&P 500 was established on March 4, 1957. The S&P 500 is not the only index fund offered by Standard and Poor company. Its selection is made by the S&P Dow Jones Indices Committee, which bases its selections of companies on many factors. The S&P 500 is market-cap-weighted, meaning that it determines the company's market capitalization by multiplying the number of shares by the price of each share. For example, if one share sells at $10, and there are one billion shares in the market, the stock is worth ten billion dollars (cap). S&P 500 focuses on stocks with the largest market caps in the United States. Market caps refer to share price *times* how many people own shares. It is broken down into large caps, mid-size caps, and small caps. You do remember market caps, don't you? If not, go to the start of this chapter and read about market caps again.

S&P 500 Index has no specific niche in focus. It tries to cover all promising sectors in the United States economy. This is why it enlists companies across industries like information, technology, health care, energy, finance, and several others. The index's primary focus is on 500 publicly traded companies with the largest cap size on the market. This explains why it lists only the 500 largest companies on the United States Stock Market. You should begin to think of world giants domiciled in the United States. I am talking about Alphabet (Google's parent company), Berkshire Hathaway, Microsoft, Amazon, Facebook, and some 495 others.

Stop for a second and imagine how it would feel if you invest in companies like this. You are arguably assured that your funds are forever secured regardless of what happens, and you will grow in leaps and bounds. Why? You trust those companies on the list. You know too well that no matter what, they would rake in the cake, and you will receive your fair share. Warren Buffett is arguably the king when it comes to investing. How much would it cost you to buy his 1 share of his indexed stock Berkshire Hathaway A? About 33,000 dollars. Instead, invest in a more affordable index fund like the S&P 500.

Take it from Wayne Duggan, writer at yahoo news,

Just to clarify, (*NYSE:* **SPY**) is a fund that tracks the S&P 500 index. Everyone who invested in (*NYSE:* **SPY**) for ten years, made out like a bandit. 250% return from an index fund! Allow me to put something in perspective for you.

During the heat of COVID-19, the market crashed, and (*NYSE:* **SPY**) went to a devastating low of 222.95. Surprisingly enough, if you invested in (*NYSE:* **SPY**) on February 1, 2016, the share price was 193.56. That means that if you decided to invest about four years prior, the pandemic that shocked the world didn't put you in the negative. You still made money!

Here, look at the 5-year chart of (*NYSE:* **SPY**).

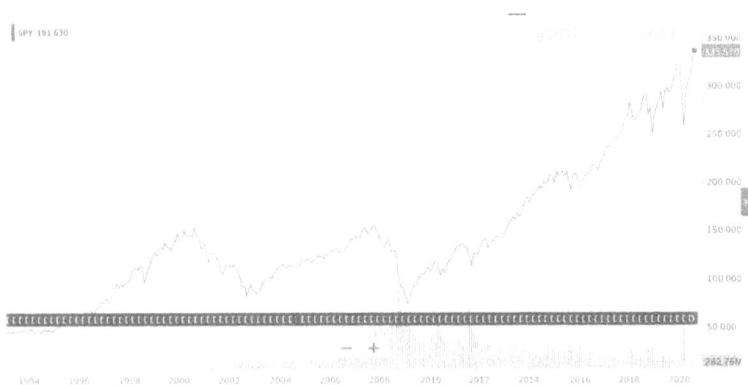

The earlier you invest, the more time the market gives you to make profits, dividends, buy more shares, and build your wealth! Truly revolutionary when you look at the performance of one index over the past few decades. Some have called the 2020 pandemic stock market crash the worst crash in recent history. In perspective, the market has been exploding with gains the past ten years that even the biggest hits from the pandemic still left people's stock in the high positive range. Remarkable stuff.

S&P 500 Index is the direct opposite of indexes like the Russell 2000 Index, which focuses on 2000 of the small-capitalization stocks on the market.

As of June 2020, the 500 companies on the S&P 500 Index issue 505 stocks. This is because companies like Google list multiple stocks on the S&P 500 constituent list. Neither the list of 500 companies nor the constituent stock list can be found on the S&P website. Only the top ten companies are listed. They are Apple Inc., Microsoft Corp, Amazon.com Inc., Facebook Inc. A., Berkshire Hathaway, JP Morgan Chase & Co., Alphabet Inc. A (Google), Alphabet Inc. B (Google), Johnson & Johnson, and Visa Inc. A. Every stock on the list is subject to replacement, depending on the financial progress of the company. So, this list is as relevant as March 2020. You can find a more extended list of companies from secondary sources but due to cap weighting, the list is subject to change.

There are strict standards to be met before a company's stock is considered in the S&P 500 index. Knowing the criteria might boost your assurances that the S&P 500 is an excellent investment choice for you. Therefore, we will briefly discuss them in the next few paragraphs.

Criteria for Enlisting in the S&P 500 Index

The requirements listed by the S&P Dow Jones Indices committee center around three factors; the *size* of the company, the *industry* or *sector* of the company, and its *liquidity*. By extension, the following factors are required:

- **Domicile**

The company should be situated in the United States. Even if it does not include all of its branches and functions in the United States, it is expected to have no less than 50% of its fixed assets in the United States. Toyota automobiles would be an excellent example of this. Toyota is diversified in the global market economy, but 50% of its fixed assets are located throughout United States territory.

- **Market cap**

S&P 500 is a market-cap-weighted index. It expects every enlisted stock to be substantially large. This implies that the company should be recognized among the largest earners in the country. The companies selected should be recognized as the most extensive stocks in its niche. Currently, the largest cap is Apple inc. ($1 trillion), while the smallest cap is Mattel Inc. ($4.2 billion). For a majority of the S&P 500 we are considering stocks with ten billion dollars and above.

- **Financial viability**

The company is expected to have made profits in 4 consecutive quarters. A company of this size that records profit in four straight quarters will likely do it again. That makes it a good investment. Profit for companies like this is not an accident. It is a result of well-executed tactics that offer long-term stability. Companies like these will likely maintain this streak for an extended period.

- **Trading and listing**

The company's stock must be listed but cannot be traded over the counter. As a rule, shares of such companies should not be traded over the counter. Most probably, everyone would focus on them if they were traded, and other investments might get insufficient consideration. All and all, the current arrangement increases the legitimacy and uniqueness of the S&P 500. Individually, each stock selected for the S&P 500 must be listed on the New York Stock Exchange, BATS Global Market, or Nasdaq.

- **Sector classification**

While the S&P 500 is not sector-specific, it tries to ensure representation across the entire United States economy. Hence, it is not surprising that it covers all major sectors. The divisions are not equally represented as you are about to see. It should not surprise you that some giant companies are sometimes switched out for other giant companies because they exist in the same sector.

As of March 2020, the Sectors of the US Economy and their representation in the S&P 500

1. Information Technology covered 24.4% of the S&P 500
2. Health Care covered 14.0%
3. Financial Corporations covered 12.2%
4. Communication Services covered 10.7%
5. Consumer Discretionary covered 9.9%
6. Industrials covered 8.9%
7. Consumer Staples covered 7.2%
8. Energy covered 3.6%
9. Utilities covered 3.5%
10. Real Estate covered 3.1%
11. Materials covered 2.5%

The figures are looking good, don't you think? This breakdown is enough proof that the S&P 500 is set up in a way that it is hard for it to fail (unless there is a total collapse of the US economy). Some of these sectors will turn out nicely, even when others underperform. Therefore, investing in the S&P 500 is an adventure that you will not regret. It is difficult to suggest or predict a number of years you need to invest to succeed because success is unmeasurable. Your standards, not mine, will determine your success. If you fall in love with the process, you will want to reinvest continuously. How does someone fall in love with investing? It's because they understand the concept of making their money work for them. When investing, you are theoretically making money as you sleep. Be patient and don't get discouraged.

How can you invest in the S&P 500?

We started this chapter by paying thorough attention to the meaning of index funds. Do you recall?

"Index mutual fund is an easy, hands-off, diversified, low-cost way to invest in the stock market."

— DAYANA YOCHIM

There are over fifty S&P 500 index funds on the market. They all have virtually identical portfolios, but the cost and tax efficiency will vary. You can contact a financial advisor or broker, but chapter 10 will show you how to set up an individual portfolio so you can get started right away. If this hasn't been made clear, you don't need anyone else's services to invest in the stock market intelligently. Having a financial advisor or a broker adds expenses that take away from your profit. Do it yourself. No one cares more about your money than you do.

The most common way the S&P 500 is traded is through an **Exchange Traded Fund (ETF)**. ETFs are very similar to indexes, but there are marked differences. We will talk about ETFs in Chapter 7.

Action To Take: Buy S&P 500 Index Fund

Highly Respectable Indexes Include:

1. Vanguard 500 Index Fund Investor Shares **(VFINX)**
2. SPDR S&P 500 ETF **(SPY)**

3. Fidelity 500 Index Fund **(FXAIX)**
4. iShares Core S&P 500 ETF **(IVV)**
5. Schwab S&P 500 Index Fund **(SWPPX)**

⁂

ENDING THOUGHTS

Now, I am sure you have pinned the S&P 500 among the top investments you will consider when you begin to gather your funds. An index like the S&P 500 guarantees return on investment when investing long-term. If you are in your 20's, the S&P 500 is a perfect index fund to invest a portion of your funds. We have not yet talked about asset allocation, but we surely will uncover its extensive benefits. We will discuss the benefits in great detail when crafting a portfolio in Chapter 10. For now, it is paramount to acknowledge allocating your assets is pairing a percentage of your cash to an investment. Assuming you invest a total of $5,000 next year, allocating 10% of your money for an S&P 500 index puts $500 into this account while leaving $4,500 in your portfolio's cash reserve. This is a great way to keep track of your investment goals and we will uncover more about this in later chapters. If the S&P 500 interests you, I would highly recommend adding it to your list of investments.

I will dive straight into the next venture. Ready to come along? Flip the page.

5
NASDAQ-100 INDEX FUND

I ndex funds are the most secure stocks in the world. We spent our last chapter on S&P 500 index funds. You will remember how safe and promising it all sounded. This time, we will thoroughly discuss another type of index, the Nasdaq-100.

Nasdaq Index Funds

National Association of Securities Dealers Automated Quotations (NASDAQ for short), was established on the 8th of February, 1971. In 1996 , NASDAQ launched the first stock exchange website in the world, www.nasdaq.com. Through its website and mobile application, it is straightforward to buy and sell stocks on an automated, transparent, and super-fast computer network. It is currently the largest Stock Exchange Market globally, right after the New Year Stock Exchange, which appears as the first.

NASDAQ released a spectacular index fund called Nasdaq-100 (abbreviated as NDX100) in 1985. It was specially designed to track the performance of the top 100 non-financial stocks that were listed on Nasdaq. By that, I mean, it is concerned about stocks that do not belong to commercial banks, credit unions, and other financial firms. As for financial stocks, Nasdaq created a separate index to track financial institutions, the NASDAQ Financial 100. You would remember that I pointed out some facts about index funds. I said it is a unique form of investment that concentrates on selected groups of stocks. The cool thing about index funds is you can track whatever portion of the market you want! There is an S&P 600 that only covers small-cap companies. Index funds pay close attention to their selected group and provide a rundown of their performance. Nasdaq-100 follows the same principle.

Nasdaq-100 began to track the most extensive stocks traded outside financial organizations. Nasdaq-100 is not particularly interested in representing every sector of the US economy. The Nasdaq-100 index fund is particularly interested in the technology sector. The fund strictly tracks the companies netting the highest profits. For the previous five years and at the start this year, 2020, technology is netting the highest profits for investors.

Financial analysts proclaim the Nasdaq-100 is more objective and goal-oriented than the S&P 500 because of Nasdaq's focus in the technology sector. They are not wrong. Technology stocks account for why Nasdaq-100 funds have recorded more success than the S&P 500.

Besides the S&P 500, Dow Jones Industrial Average is the nearest index you can compare the Nasdaq-100 with. They are regarded as the big three. Nasdaq-100 is also traded as Invesco QQQ, in the Exchange Trade Fund (ETF). I assure you, we will talk about ETFs later.

We clearly understand that the Nasdaq-100 is an index stock, which implies it will likely yield profits across bullish sectors. Yet, we need to get our hands on some basic facts before investing. The same way we did with the S&P 500.

What is the Primary Objective of Nasdaq-100 Index Funds?

The main goal of Nasdaq-100 index funds is to compile stocks that beat its previous performance. Nasdaq tries to guarantee a reliable investment in all of its stocks. You want to remember that, like the S&P 500, Nasdaq's stocks are not fixed. They are altered according to the market impression of the company.

I will explain how the Nasdaq-100 works for you. Nasdaq selects many companies that offer dividends to investors. Some of the companies may not yield dividends, but many others do. Besides, it has performed impressively on all counts. It has even generated more than the S&P 500, which integrates up to 400 dividend-paying stocks.

Nasdaq-100 has 100 target companies that currently list 103 stocks. This makes it easy to invest in more than one stock, thereby diversifying your funds. It is pretty similar to how the S&P 500 operates. It only looks superior because it diversifies extra assurance; you are one of the companies' owners, and you stand to make more profit. Besides, it has proven to be as reliable as the S&P 500 over the past twelve years.

Nasdaq-100 is cap-weighted like the S&P 500. Nasdaq-100 selects the top 100 companies with the largest caps. The Nasdaq-100 index likes to diversify in a few sectors but not all of them. This is why the 100 large cap companies selected are not the top 100 large caps in the world. Rather, they are 100 large cap companies in chosen sectors of the market. These companies span across technology, healthcare, consumer services, and some others. The companies selected are domestic and international; at least five foreign companies are on their current list. You can read over the complete list of companies on Nasdaq's official website.

As a rule of thumb, Nasdaq-100, S&P 500, and Down Jones Industrial Average (also known as Dow), share many similarities. Why? Because they are all index funds! All index funds have a lot in common because they diversify their funds across the market to achieve a rounded profit for their investors.

3 Reasons You should Consider Investing in a Nasdaq-100 Index Fund

- **Diversification of funds**

All index funds offer more than one stock. It allows investors to invest in more than one stock with every index fund they purchase. This feature can be advantageous since it offers the opportunity to partake in a large group of stocks that buyers don't always consider.

Nasdaq-100 is among the most significant diversified index funds in the United States. It coves much as a hundred different companies with an excellent track record and enormous potential. Each company operates on a separate system, and they have different targets. Facebook, Google, and Amazon are kings of the internet, no doubt. They may all be classified as web-based companies, but it is pretty clear that they operate differently. So, most of the firms on the list are compiled together under the name "technology."

By the way, these companies are among the most successful companies in the world. The four companies in the world that have hit a trillion-dollar net worth are listed here (Apple, Amazon, Alphabet, and Microsoft). Cross investing in these giants is a sure way to make plenty of money. As long as your wealth is growing, who cares what the sector is? Like the S&P 500, Nasdaq-100 has a proven record of success with its diversification over unpredictable single company stock.

- **Track record**

Going by fundamental analysis, Nasdaq-100 is one of the most profitable index funds on the market. The record has shown that between 2003 to 2020, it has consistently yielded 24% earnings and 14% revenue. It also has yielded up to a 20% dividend. Because bullish statistics took place in the past, does not mean the Nasdaq-100 will perform this way each year in the future. The most crucial thing to remember is, if you buy and hold long-term, your wealth will surely grow. You may, of course, consider your technical analysis. But the fundamental analysis has shown that you can hit your big financial dreams with a fund that has done it repeatedly.

Nasdaq-100 has been successful; it has recorded tremendous success against its closest contemporaries, the Dow Jones and the S&P 500. Whether you desire to consider its dividend, value, price, or annual earnings, the Nasdaq-100 has excelled in all of these sections.

- **Prospect**

It is not enough to only rely on an impressive past. A proper investment must show signs of an explosive future too. The prospect of Nasdaq-100 is the most important weapon I can hand to you at the moment. As an investor, it is something that can be your compass to success in the next ten years. What am I talking about? Pure analysis.

As of June 2020, pundits predict that the Nasdaq-100 has more upside potential than the S&P 500. Larry Fink, BlackRock's CEO, observes that people are using technology more than ever. Due to the global lockdown from March 2020, more people have been stuck in their homes. They have made daily use of information technologies like social media. They have tried software like Zoom to foster their work from home. People are playing video games, ordering more from online stores, making an excessive amount of digital payments, and so on. The lockdown has accelerated many of these activities due to the accessibility of technology. The technology boom will not go away, either. Technology growth will continue long after the lockdown or COVID-19 is over. This indicates that Nasdaq-100, which targets technology, will continuously experience a substantial shift in growth over the next few months, years, and decades. As long as the world's market economy stays open, the world's investors will profit from it.

Nasdaq-100 does not only consider consumer technology. The health and biotech sector has a significant impact on the Nasdaq-100's upside potential as well. A few health and biotech companies are testing for various cures such as a COVID-19 vaccine. This could theoretically change the market cap forever if a company finds and properly distributes a cure for the virus in the form of a vaccine.

Consumer consumption companies make up about 17% of Nasdaq-100 stocks. Pepsi, Netflix, Starbucks, and several others are among the companies represented in Nasdaq.

The world is fast developing, and technology sits at the helm of the global revolution. New technology facilities are being designed and constructed every day. This is all proof that Nasdaq-100 has an impressive past, and it holds a promising future for anyone willing to stake its risks.

How to Invest in Nasdaq-100

As an index, Nasdaq-100 can be accessed in several ways. It can be accessed as an Invesco (**QQQ**), and an Exchange Traded Fund, which I will tell you all about in the following pages. Already, Invesco is about to be the most traded ETF in the United States. In the past five years alone, **QQQ** has had a market increase of over 150%. It can also be traded as options and annuities.

In chapter 10, I have documented an easy way to get acquainted with all of these stock options. In addition, there will be an outline of a step by step guide on how to get started with investing in the stock market. You will not only see them in action, but you will also learn how they operate. You can invest confidently without the help of a stockbroker or a financial advisor. These services are not needed. Do advisors help? Yes, they do, but they are not worth the expense in the modern era of trading. Imagine making 7% a year from your investments, but instead, you only receive half because of a financial advisor fee. The basic formula and decisions a financial advisor makes to gain profits for you and his company are thoroughly detailed throughout this book. Advice from books and the free information on the internet will do just fine. When you are ready to invest and make one of the most significant long-term life-changing decisions you will ever make, see Chapter 10.

We have discussed a great deal about Nasdaq-100 and S&P 500. I realize it may confuse you, and you may be riddled with indecision. To help you through that, I will consider a succinct analysis by putting these two investments side by side.

Differences Between Nasdaq-100 and S&P 500 Index Funds

As the record has proven, Nasdaq-100 is much different from the S&P 500 index funds. Although these two powerhouses are entangled in many of the same sectors, there are significant differences. They are as follows:

- **Economy**

These indexes bear little semblance on the sectors they target. Nasdaq-100 is generally listed as a technology index. Up to 50% of the Nasdaq-100 stocks span across pure technology and information technology firms. For the S&P 500, however, efforts are made to represent the US economy as much as possible. You might have noticed this in the previous chapter, where we listed some of the S&P prominent sectors.

Notwithstanding, some stocks crisscross and are found in both indexes, notably, companies like Apple Inc., Facebook Inc., Microsoft, and others. As an investor, the sectors targeted in the economy should be something you are concerned about. If financial institutions are flourishing, you will not see immediate growth when investing your funds in the Nasdaq-100. Nasdaq-100 does not track financial institutions. You will see growth in your portfolio from the Nasdaq-100, but it will be over time, hence the strategy of long-term investing. Good things come to those who wait. **Diversification is key.** You can grow your wealth with both (Nasdaq-100 and the S&P 500) if you patiently wait for the economy to manifest its cycle.

- **Target size**

Just as its name suggests, Nasdaq-100 tailors its benchmark on the largest 100 stocks of non-financial institutions. 50% borders around healthcare, consumer services, industrial, and bio-techs. A whopping 50% belongs to technology-based companies. In another way, the S&P 500 set its benchmark on the top 500 companies in the country. Most sectors are included if you engage in the S&P 500.

Besides this, S&P offers a much larger diversification, making it possible to own shares and stock in more companies than you could otherwise have managed individually. The Nasdaq-100 provides this too. But it is at a 20% rate of what the S&P 500 does. This should not affect you as an investor. If you have always longed to specialize in fast-growing, high tech firms, Nasdaq offers enough diversification to fit your needs.

- **Stock variety**

We have earlier pointed out that there are varying kinds

of stocks. Both Nasdaq-100 and the S&P 500 offer a variety of stocks. A large percentage of Nasdaq-100 stocks are common. By implication, they generate percentage ownership of the companies involved. This means that the dividend is non-compulsory. Nonetheless, the companies are fast-growing, profitable, and well-established; thus, they offer dividends comfortably. This explains why Nasdaq-100 could yield up to 20% in dividends over twenty years.

Similarly, the S&P 500 is a blend of companies that offer both common and preferred stocks. Since the S&P 500 invests in large corporations, many companies provide dividends, even when investing in them through common stocks. As of March 2020, up to 400 stocks in the S&P 500 offer dividends. Regardless, Nasdaq-100 has yielded more earnings, dividends, and interest than the S&P 500 in the last decade. This trend is subject to change with time.

- **Volatility**

Volatility refers to the rate at which a stock appears risky. It refers to how high or low the risks involved are. Usually, volatility explains how fast declines can happen in the value of a stock, leading to losses. You will want to remember that the Nasdaq-100 is more volatile than the S&P 500. The implication is that, with Nasdaq only covering 100 companies, the volatility is greater than the S&P 500 stocks. The fewer number of stocks included in an index usually transpires to more volatility. The top ten stocks of Nasdaq-100 are among the largest companies in the world. Alone, they constitute more than half of the value of Nasdaq-100 stocks.

The implication of volatility is that price alteration or change in the market can swing any of these companies, which will rock the Nasdaq-100 stock price and value (short-term). A bit unlike this, S&P 500 diversifies to more sectors than Nasdaq. It also constitutes large companies whose prices may slightly affect its value. Despite this, it is stable and less volatile than the Nasdaq-100.

Let us consider some real experiences. Nasdaq-100 rose by 130% in 1999 with a sudden upsurge in the use of technology. S&P 500 only increased by 11%. In March 2000, the Nasdaq-100 abruptly fell by 67%, while the S&P 500 fell by only 23%. More statistical data can prove the volatility of the trends and patterns, but this is enough to point out the basic theory to you regarding a comparison of volatility. In the future, Nasdaq-100 will continue to be more volatile than the S&P 500. Nasdaq offers bigger up-swings and larger down-swings than the S&P 500.

Despite its volatility, Nasdaq-100 has yielded more profits over ten of the past twelve years for investors.

- **Past**

Do investors rely on the performance of the past when predicting the future of the market? Some do, but then, I must warn you. When looking at statistical data that analyzes the Nasdaq-100 index's performance versus the S&P 500 index, all the facts suggest that Nasdaq-100 is the top dog. Nasdaq-100 has steadily risen while turning in more results than the S&P 500. Based on market records, Nasdaq-100 has yielded more returns than its close contenders like Russell 1000 and the S&P 500.

The statistics of the past do not guarantee the future. Because this book focuses on seven handpicked investments,

I would have to recommend purchasing both indexes as this will ensure you a more diversified portfolio.

- **Potential**

As I have pointed out to you on the last page, Nasdaq-100 holds every potential for excellence. It lists companies and sectors that will strive to recuperate from the global pandemic quickly and get in shape for better performances again. Of course, every industry will try to increase performance, but some have higher chances of success because they are essential amenities to the world. I am describing sectors like consumer services, industrials, healthcare, aviation, and the brightest of all, technology.

On the other hand, the S&P 500 does not center on technology. It includes many companies and sectors that have been severely affected by the current standstill in business transactions. Travel, clothing, oils, and many others industries were critically hit during lockdown. It might take them a few years to come full circle and bounce back to prosperous businesses. Some of these firms may not pick up soon. Investors may not receive yields, and possibly, run into a loss. As long as these sectors are reflected in the S&P 500, investing in it remains a tricky choice for strategic investors like you. Although, it is essential to look at the potential of an index or a stock for two reasons. Reason one, after looking at the companies and sectors the index or stock represents, you will have a good idea where the index or stock is headed. Reason two, when a stock or index is undervalued that is the time to buy!

If the market crashes, look at it as an opportunity. If you are fearful of the market's future, confidently hold. An intelligent investor, who is young and plans to invest for 20+ years, would buy up thousands of dollars in stock when there is a market crash. Buy stock on sale, sell stock when it reaches its peak. Although every situation has its specificity, these principles will serve you well for years to come.

All that said, I am confident that you can now differentiate Nasdaq-100 from the S&P 500. I will leave you to process the information, take into account the present time we live in, and settle upon your decisions. I also advise that you consider a thorough analysis of the trend, especially if you are reading this guide decades beyond 2020. Analysis of the current market can help you weigh your chances of success or failure. In case you are not sure how to go about that, I have written it in the next few lines.

Market Analysis

Market Analysis is a deliberate effort to research and figure out which investments have high potential. It is factual, empirical, and prospective research that can tell you what kind of stocks work best towards your investing goals. Briefly, there are two types of market analysis.

- **Fundamental analysis**

Fundamental analysis is an attempt to understand the company's stock by its surrounding circumstances. You are trying to determine what factors play into the performance of the stock, and how the price per share can be affected. For example, you may be interested in finding out the economic, social, or industry factors that may influence the stock's value. In the end, the stock may be considered undervalued or overvalued at its current price. These variables lose their importance the longer you invest your money in the market. Allow most of these ticky-tack variables to slip your mind while you put your nose to the grindstone and continue investing long-term.

- **Technical analysis**

Technical analysis is a form of commentary that bases its analysis on past experiences. Let me make it clear. Sometimes, you can determine the chances of a market swing by reviewing its history. This is the same concept when pundits predict a sports team's performance based on the team's previous record and stats. You can conveniently predict a machine's expected performance based on its previous performance. You are certainly not judging by a single experience. Your decisions will be based on steady performances over long-term statistical data.

Similarly, you can predict the prospect of stock by considering its antecedents. "How has it always been done?" You might ask yourself, "what are the prospects of better performance?" "Will this trend continue?" "When is the best time for entry or exit?"

Carrying out such research on stocks can boost your chances of improved yields in the stock market.

Action To Take: Buy Nasdaq-100 Index Fund

Highly Respectable Indexes Include:

1. Invesco QQQ Trust **(QQQ)**
2. ProShares UltraPro QQQ **(TQQQ)**

3. ProShares Ultra QQQ **(QLD)**
4. USAA Nasdaq-100 Index Fund **(USNQX)**
5. Fidelity Nasdaq Composite Index Tracking Stock ETF **(ONEQ)**

ENDING THOUGHTS

In this chapter, we discussed the pros and cons of investing in the Nasdaq-100. As you can tell, I am an avid fan of index funds like the S&P 500 and Nasdaq-100. The reason is simple. Index funds will assure long-term success in the market by spreading your money across 100 companies, in the case of our Nasdaq index fund, and 500 companies, in the case of our S&P index fund.

It has been made clear; Nasdaq-100 holds massive potential for you as a long-term investor. It demands some level of risk, but it has excelled greatly ten out of the last twelve years. The 100 companies involved in the Nasdaq-100 index fund diversifies across a large portion of the market and would be a great investment decision for someone looking to invest their money long-term. Long-term investors buy and hold, reinvest their dividends, and watch their wealth surge. The five index trackers listed above have differences so it would be a good idea to do individual research on them. USAA Nasdaq-100 Index Fund **(USNQX)** is the only stock listed above that is not traded on Robinhood. You can find **(USNQX)** on Fidelity. The other four are found on most all platforms. Even Fidelity's Nasdaq Composite Index Tracking Stock ETF **(ONEQ)**, is found on Robinhood and other brokerage sites.

6

A HANDS OFF APPROACH WITH MUTUAL FUNDS

I s the stock market making no sense to you, but you still want to invest?

Okay. I have a great idea. I have a couple of friends who can't get into stocks either. They do not hate the system. Rather, they cannot figure out how it all works. More importantly, they are too busy with their life, and they do not want to take time out of their day to make decisions. It sounds like a dark, awkward wall every time anyone mentions the stock market to them. It is quite possible that you feel this way too. Should you then force yourself into a market, you don't seem ever to understand? Probably not.

"Never invest in a market you do not understand."

— WARREN BUFFETT

Yet, you want to invest because investing is a key to

multiplying your wealth. What is the way to go for you then? Easy. A mutual fund is the answer.

Mutual Funds

According to FBN, a financial institution, a mutual fund is a medium of investing that allows many people to pool their resources together and invest. A mutual fund typically happens where people who have common goals meet and collate their assets. For example, you and fifty other people, who are about your age and financial status, may combine your funds and invest in fixed income funds. You likely will not see any of these people or ever know their names. A fund manager does the collation. No rule says these other fifty people have to be of your age or financial status. It is just typical for people to be grouped in this way because they usually have similar financial goals.

A mutual fund is a medium through which you team up with other people, combine your resources, and invest in promising assets, treasury bills, bonds, stocks, and so on. Stocks again? Yes. An investment in stocks is one of the most promising solutions. You do not have to worry. A mutual fund can be managed by a team of experts that make investment decisions for you. You do not have to do the thinking or selection; you simply pay the funds.

"Mutual funds have historically offered safety and diversification. And they spare you the responsibility of picking individual stocks."

— RON CHERNOW

Expansively, a mutual fund is a fund collated by fund managers. These fund managers are usually recognized as financial institutions such as banks, brokerage companies, et cetera. They typically have enough experience and expertise to make business decisions for a large number of people and funds. You need to make sure that your potential fund manager is a specialist who has a good track record. You certainly want your investments to yield as much as possible, and experience can teach people "how".

Adam Hayes notes that participating in mutual funds is usually open to the whole world. There is a typical range of prices that each participant may select from. This minimum amount is generally meager, which makes it a saving grace for really low-income earners to invest a little amount of money. By way of illustration, the minimum amount set for participation maybe $15, while the maximum is $150. This means you may invest only $15 as a participant or any other amount that falls below $150. Undoubtedly, you can invest $150 too. Though, sometimes there is no deposit limit. Do not worry if you do not have $10,000 to invest. Start small in the beginning and increase your investments later if you desire.

The company places your money into an investment. You have a unit (a percentage according to your contribution) of whatever the mutual fund is invested in. The financial manager decides how best to invest the funds, and they often consider bonds, assets, and stocks. Your money manager will likely consider investing in more than one type. Usually, the individual investor knows close to nothing about the processes of investment taken on by the money manager. You are provided regular information on the nature of the investment and the rise or fall of the fund value.

The value of the mutual fund is determined by the stocks or securities the money manager chooses for you. As an illustration, let us presume a mutual fund is gathered to purchase three stocks; Nasdaq-100, the S&P 500, and the Russell 3000. If the value of these stocks fall due to a pandemic, social, or psychological factor, you and your fund manager will be affected.

The rise or fall of the stock value will determine the yield of given to each investor. Also, participants in mutual funds bear equal risks and benefits. There is equal representation, and each participant is compensated according to how much they contribute in a fair proportion.

A mutual fund investment strategy is congruent with many other styles of investing. It is very similar to the way index's diversity funds. Some people even classify an index as a mutual fund. The difference is that a mutual fund is not a direct investment in any stock, and there are no voting rights in this situation. You are in for yields and interest only. One other thing, stocks are not the only form of investments considered in mutual funds. Bonds, securities, treasury bills, and similar investments are all considered.

When Does a Mutual Fund Generate Profit?

The profit rate of a mutual fund occurs in two situations.

1. When the security yields dividends
2. When the value of the stock increases

More often than not, the two cases are guaranteed in every mutual fund investment. It is because the fund is being handled by an expert money manager who will play the market to avoid losses. If you make money, so does the money manager. They will diversify the accumulated funds so that one of their investments should yield if another does not. FBN, a financial institution, notes this in one of their guides to mutual fund investment. They do this for a living. They are expected to be proficient in their trade

There is one fact you should know, in any case. The dividend is usually low. You may yield little over a long period. If you aim to build a future with mutual funds, you will need a great deal of patience. Lucky for people in their 20's, time and patience are on your side, so use your discretion wisely.

I recommend high paying dividend stocks and index funds because they typically yield steady profit over the long haul. Mutual fund investments are ideal for the hands off investor to set up a reacquiring investment and forgetting their investment exists. For someone not interested in actively managing your portfolio, mutual funds are for you.

Types of Mutual Funds

Earlier, I drew attention to the fact that a fund manager may invest in more than one option. The options available to a fund manager will be determined by the type of mutual funds you have selected. So, what are the types of mutual funds that you or your money manager may choose from?

- **Bond/fixed – income mutual funds**

Bond or fixed income mutual funds are among the most popular mutual funds in the market. As the Investment Company Institute (ICI) observes, it accounts for no less than 20% of the mutual funds in the stock market. This means that one of every five persons in mutual funds prefer bond mutual funds.

Unlike equity mutual funds, which consider stocks, fixed income investments focus on bonds. Bond/fixed income mutual funds are invested across government bonds, corporate bonds, and so on.

Bond income mutual funds are considered one of the most reliable forms of investment. They yield steady income and there are fewer risks. This makes bond income mutual funds a lot more predictable than fixed income mutual funds. It is ideal for anyone worried about the unpredictable swings of the marketplace. I recommend this to you if you are in your 30's or 40's. This type for investment is stable, keeping your money secure with small amounts of volatility.

If you are in your 20's however, I insist that an equity mutual fund is the best type of mutual fund you can ever consider. More risk, more reward. But what if you are looking for stability with minimal risk? Why should you take on so much uncertainty when there is less risk and some assurance elsewhere? It is simple. Bond mutual funds offer a low risk. But they provide low rates too. Their yields are so low it won't impress someone in their youth. If you are in your 20's, you should feel comfortable taking big risks. Equity mutual funds have risks, but they have very appealing returns. Equity mutual funds need years to grow before showing a consistent profit. For someone in their 20's, time is something you have a lot of. I had always believed that Alex Berenson was thinking about us when he said that,

"The thing to do with mutual funds is to buy a couple of decent ones, set up an investment plan and then never, ever think, about them again, except maybe once a quarter or so when you take a peek at your statements to make sure that you have not accidentally been buying the fidelity peace-in-the-middle-east fund."

— ALEX BERENSON

Besides being very comedic, Alex has the right idea. Someone in their 20's can invest in an equity mutual fund, let it sit for many years, and receive the reward without doing anything extra!

- **Stock/equity mutual funds**

Stock or equity mutual funds are the most common type of mutual fund in the stock market. According to the Investment Company Institute, stock mutual funds alone constitute up to 55% of all mutual funds. This means they are vastly available and considered satisfactory by most mutual fund investors. Strangely, all statistics suggest that they are riskier than most others. You have to be prepared for swings and surprises if you are considering this type of investment.

Equity or stock mutual funds are invested in the shares of companies and organizations. Such companies are selected according to specific criteria, and the fund manager largely determines whether to invest in them or not. Companies that hire fund managers are always striving to get better and yield higher returns. Of course, there is still an off chance that a fund manager will mismanage your investments. A good thing to remember is that there are no guarantees. Although the probability is high that your fund manager will give you good ROI, you are taking a chance when someone else manages your money. Not to mention the expense rate you will pay for their service.

- **Money market mutual funds**

Money market mutual funds are a form of mutual funds that make efforts to invest in steady assets. It invests in stable assets that can generate profits for investors while maintaining the main fund. They are usually high quality and short-term. Treasury bills, commercial papers, and the US certificate of deposit are common examples of such funds.

They are less popular than the previously described mutual funds. However, they constitute up to 15% of the mutual fund market, and they are just for you if you are in your later years.

- **Multi-asset or balanced mutual funds**

This is an all-compassing type of investment. It is a form of mutual funds that include every item we have highlighted in the previous instances. Specifically, equity, fixed income, treasury bills, commercial papers, and so on are all considered in the form of a mutual fund.

There are a variety of balanced mutual funds in varying ratios—for instance, 70% equity, 20% fixed income, and 10% money market. You do not want to forget that this is a mere illustration; there is a wide variety of multi asset funds available. My studies have revealed that despite its diversification, only a negligible percentage of investors invest in multi-asset or balanced mutual funds. This should not keep you away. You may consider it alongside your equity investment.

Now that you understand the various kinds of mutual funds available, we may discuss another crucial point. What do you need to know before selecting your mutual fund? There are factors you need to consider when choosing a mutual fund. It is crucial to understand you do not need to pay a broker or a financial advisor to invest your money successfully. Doing so will lower your total return. Whether you decide to hire a professional or do it yourself, use the factors below before selecting a mutual fund that best fits your interests. I am confident that after you flip the final page in this book, your decision making in the stock market will be more than satisfactory.

Some of the Standard Criteria that Your Money Manager may Consider Before Selecting a Stock Mutual Fund

- **Location of the firm**

Kevin Voight, one of the best investment analysts in the United States, points out that location is a crucial factor for mutual fund investments. Choosing the right location can increase your chances of a better investment. There are usually three options to select from; international stocks, global stocks, and emerging market funds. International stocks are stocks of firms that are not in the United States. However, global stocks are traded in the United States and worldwide. Your financial manager may consider it ideal to invest in stocks that have a versatile market. Also, emerging companies outside the United States could be excellent for young entrepreneurs looking to diversify their portfolio. In particular, these companies have a high tendency to grow and yield dividends. Every firm has the propensity to generate satisfactory profits.

If you would like to diversify your portfolio with a stock from China, where do you start? Perhaps, look at a sector that is currently flourishing in China. An example of a sector that is blossoming in China right now is the delivery service from suppliers to consumers. In the United States, this service is lead by UPS in the private sector. ZTO Express **(ZTO)** is a Chinese company transporting products from supplier warehouses right to the consumer's doorstep. ZTO Express has done an impressive job implementing UPS's blueprint in delivering high quality service to the citizens of China. This would be an example of a company located outside the United States that has potential upside. Notwithstanding, it is very important to check the company's financial records. If a global/foreign company has recorded profits for the past eight quarters and has met the requirements to qualify the stock as a good investment, take a swing at it.

- **Industry**

The industry is another determining factor that helps a fund manager decide where to dispense funds. As the world is fast expanding, several sectors are witnessing a larger boom than ever and holding a prosperous future for investors. As an example, companies in the technology and BioTech industry are growing faster than ever. Some would consider the age we are currently living in as the technological revolution. On the flip side, companies in art and aesthetics are declining, and their stock price shows it. The demand for the art industry has had a negative shift in the past decade (2010-2020). If I had to guess, it is because other sectors like technology and biotech have been the front runners in the past decade. There is just more demand for technology and less need for art and aesthetics.

However, this does not make sectors and industries on the decline unworkable in your stock portfolio. Your fund manager may be tactical with your investment, and they might hit even the declining industry with the right timing. Aesthetics in the gaming industry are at an all-time demand due to the progression of graphics. The principle here is, do not rely on one statistic to examine an entire field.

> **Side Note:** *When sitting down with a fund manager, they will generally lay out a whole bunch of options you can invest in and let you pick your desired sectors/industries. Your industry of choice is an excellent starting point. It is crucial to comprehend the sector(s) you want to invest your money in for the next 20+ years.*

- **Company size**

The company is another determining factor in mutual fund selection. We might say, this is not just for mutual funds, but all investments. Consider the company size upon your selection. What is the capitalization size (small-cap, mid-cap or large-cap)? An abridged way you can quickly identify the size of a company is to look at its cap-size. You can easily do this by making an internet search.

- **Growth or value orientation**

Growth companies are companies looking to expand at the slightest opportunity. Adams Hayes submitted in a 2019 research paper that growth companies may pay little or no dividends. They usually make profits, but the company reinvests a large percentage of their gains into expanding the company, rather than reinvesting the extra money in the pockets of the shareholders.

Growth companies have a high tendency to shoot up over the coming years. These companies are hopeful that investors don't mind them reinvesting their money back into the company instead of in the form of dividends.

Value-oriented companies are well established. They are concerned about providing benefits to customers, investors, and the company alike. They are not particular about growth anymore. Hence, a higher percentage of profit is paid to investors through dividends.

The criteria your money manager considers before selecting mutual funds should be the same criteria you consider. As an investor, it is highly profitable that you know where your investments are going. Putting all the previous information into perspective, you as the investor can decide your best choice for equity mutual funds, and ransack the market. Examination is the most crucial step in executing a great plan. The tactics to go about your research are here. Use it at your disposal.

Factors to Consider Before Selecting a Mutual Fund

- **Type of investment**

The first factor to be considered is the type and style of the available mutual funds. Be certain that the mutual fund is low-risk, long or short-term, et cetera. You have to be sure that whatever you opt for aligns perfectly with your goals.

- **Previous performance of funds**

You want to determine whether these funds have performed impressively or weakly. You want to know which of the available funds have an impeccable past and a promising future. Though, an impressive history does not guarantee the future. Nevertheless, it may be a good indication that a mutual fund is established and will continue to succeed. Look at past profits and identify if the profits recorded are stable. If profits fell in the negative during a few quarter's, ask yourself why this happened. Was there a shift in the company's CEO? Did the company go through a merger that was unsuccessful? Is the product they are selling outdated? These are all questions you should ask if a company is recording a loss.

- **Fund manager's experience**

According to an investment analyst at *Cowrywise*, the fund manager is the most important element in mutual fund investment. He/She is the person who decides the best steps to take at each moment, what to invest in, or what to specifically avoid. The importance of this individual cannot be overemphasized. His/Her singular actions may lead to the success or failure of the mutual fund. As such, you need to doubly verify that your fund manager has a track record of making waves with mutual funds, particularly the type of mutual fund you have selected.

- **Expense ratio**

Expense ratio refers to the fees that are accrued to managing and maintaining your funds. This is usually determined by the firm managing your money. You do not want to incur an expense ratio that makes it impossible to yield any noteworthy gain from your investment. If you are assured that your expense ratio would be negligible compared to your yields, you may consider overlooking the expense cost. I have been invested in stocks with a 1% expense ratio and I have been invested in stocks with a 0.04% expense ratio. The stock's performance minus the expense ratio determines your profit

- **Exit load**

Exit load typically refers to the amount you receive from your investment yields. It refers to the total amount you are permitted to withdraw from the yields of the transaction. For example, you may be allowed up to 50% of your returns as your exit load. Many others offer less. The important thing to remember is that the lower your exit load, the better for your investment.

Top Reasons for Recommending Mutual Funds

- **Asset segregation**

One of the most assuring points about mutual funds is they are segregated. The instant you deposit your funds in a mutual fund investment, it is separated from your other financial transactions. It is also separated from the other assets or resources of your brokerage company. This way, it is easy to trace the progress and movement of your funds.

- **Diversification**

Diversification is one of the only ways to guarantee that your portfolio does not take a severe hit and go down the drain. Even if some of your funds do not yield your desired results, you are certain others will.

- **Regular updates**

If you have a fund manager, you should be duly updated on the progress of your portfolio every quarter, six months, or year. Your fund manager will update you, and the updates will be detailed enough to help you decide the trend which your investments might follow in the coming period. If you are making a direct investment, it is no one's job to update you besides yourself. Investing in stocks on your own is easily manageable. Setting aside an hour every two weeks to update yourself is a great habit.

- **Liquidity**

Liquidity refers to your ability to dispense your investments and quickly receive your funds. In other words, selling stock. Once in a while, you may have reasons to dump your current investment and try something new. You may also be financially stuck to the point where you need to sell some stock to pay for an emergency. A mutual fund is one of the most reliable funds in this regard. You can sell off your investment and get your funds processed within a few business days.

- **Simplicity/flexibility**

If you are looking for the most comfortable way to save for the future, and hands-off, a mutual fund is a fantastic option. You are neither bothered about picking the fund(s) (If you decide to hire an advisor) or maintaining the stocks. With an expert fund manager, you can drop your funds and disappear. Or, do it on your own. You can't disappear in the traditional sense, but with a few hours every three months, you can successfully manage your own mutual fund. It is easier than it sounds, and I hope all of the information provided about mutual funds will make you feel confident to take the route of managing your own mutual fund/portfolio.

The benefit of managing your own mutual fund/portfolio is that you can maximize your investment returns.

"I have mutual funds. I have a lot of individual stocks. I am across the board. Really well-diversified."

— DUFF MCKAGAN

Sound like something you should try? It is, trust me.

Action To Take: Buy a Mutual Fund

Highly Respectable Mutual Funds Include:

1. Fidelity Small-Cap Growth Fund **(FCPGX)**
2. Blackstone Group **(BX)**
3. JPMorgan Large Cap Growth R5 **(JLGRX)**
4. T. Rowe Price Dividend Growth **(PRDGX)**
5. American Funds American Mutual Fund Class A **(AMRMX)**

ENDING THOUGHTS

Mutual funds are an easy, hands off solution to growing your money. There are only so many hours in a day and people have different hobbies. In the few extra hours you have every night after work, you may enjoy water painting, jamming out on your drum set to a new song, or watching your favorite show on Netflix. Spending the small amount of free time you have every night learning about financial literacy… extremely boring to a majority of people. So instead, take the knowledge you have discovered so far, find a few promising funds, set up a recurring investment through your bank (see Chapter 10), and let your wealth compound and never ever think about it again. Truly, this is a guaranteed way to build wealth without constantly thinking about how your investments are performing.

Having said that, what if you are the person who refuses to settle for average. If you would like to make more than a few percent a year on your investments and take a more assertive approach, flip the page. Another exciting investment awaits.

7

THE EXCHANGE-TRADED FUND (ETF)

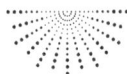

"An Exchange Traded Fund is an investment vehicle, a hybrid of mutual funds and closed-end funds."

— KEN FAULKENBERRY

Okay. I am going to agree with you. This guy speaks in riddles, but I can break it down better. Ken Faulkenberry is pointing out that ETFs are a medium of investment. It is another system through which you invest your funds in the stock market. It is a combination of mutual and closed-end funds. Think of ETFs as index funds. You are not choosing to invest in one company but rather hundreds. I will break down what an ETF means, but it can be complex. The easiest way I understand an ETF is that I compare it to an index fund because it is a diverse trading platform. If you remember the way a mutual funds work, you have a good idea where we are heading already, since a closed-end fund is another variant of mutual funds.

In different words, an ETF is a type of investment that involves a collection of securities and stocks. The investment type tracks an underlying index too. An ETF collects securities and tracks indexes. Additionally, an ETF invests in collectibles, stocks, bonds, and so on. Then, it breaks its total worth down into shares. Individual investors buy these stocks or shares.

Cash Invested in ETFs

The dollar amount, in trillions, invested in exchange-traded funds worldwide.

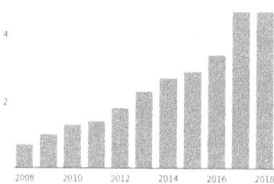

Source: ETFGI

An ETF is another way to gather funds together and invest in shares and stocks across diverse fields. The larger the index that is tracked by the ETF, the broader it's diversification. You are directly in charge of purchasing your shares. Experts insist that ETFs are an advanced form of mutual funds.

An engaging fact is that you may directly purchase or sell ETF shares at any time in the stock market. They are traded like regular stocks. You can always access your funds when you sell. Some brokerage sites like Robinhood will instantly give you your money, while other brokerages like Computershare will take more time processing your order. Depending on your brokerage, you could wait up to a month or more to get your money.

In the case of ETFs, you could buy, sell, buy, and sell as much as you want every day on the stock market. You can buy as little as $5 and hold for as low as one minute. I do not mean that you should sell your stocks like a day trader. I am only pointing out that the ETF market has high liquidity.

From the chart displayed above, you will agree that ETFs have seen impressive growth over time.

Like many other stock options, investors get dividends and annual reports on their investment performance. As stipulated by the Investment Company Act of 1940, every new ETF has to be endorsed by the Securities and Exchange Commission (SEC). Overall, ETFs take the same format as a mutual fund, but it is a newer form that offers some tantalizing features. To be sure we don't get confused, we first need to talk about their similarities.

The Similarities Between ETFs and Mutual Funds

- **Both hold a portfolio of stocks**

As we have pointed out while discussing mutual funds, ETFs also invest in several stocks and indexes. Both can purchase or invest in similar securities. As such, they are not so different in their operation. It is why indexes like the S&P 500 can be traded as mutual funds or ETFs. Many stocks on the market can be traded under the umbrella of a mutual fund or an ETF.

- **Diversification**

Diversification is a crucial element we have discussed throughout the book. The reason why diversification keeps getting brought up repeatedly is that it is a top 10 formula for successful long-term investing. With diversification, a sector in the market can fall, but the others will stabilize your earnings. It is beneficial to own ETFs and mutual funds because diversification acts as a fail-safe.

A lot of striking lines exist between ETFs and Mutual Funds. Recognizing how they are different should be a fundamental concern.

What are the Distinguishing Differences Between Mutual Funds and ETFs?

- **No assistance needed from a fund manager**

If you invest in a mutual fund, you do not have direct transactions with the stocks or their companies. You simply purchase a portion of the mutual fund and hands-off. This means that after your financial contribution, the bulk of the assignment falls on your fund manager. This is not the same when purchasing an ETF. You are solely responsible for the purchase of an ETF. You are directly purchasing from the seller, and as such, a manager has close to nothing to do with ETF trading. This is good because it allows you to cut out many middleman expenses. This means more money in your pocket. Though, you will still spend a low expense ratio of 0.44% annually (on average). That should translate to $4.40 on a $1000 investment. You could have spent that at your favorite coffee shop yesterday. Cheap stuff.

- **ETF is an intraday trade**

One feature of mutual funds is that they cannot be purchased until the market is over for the day. They are not traded on stock exchanges; you would remember that you can only purchase them from brokers (fidelity.com is an example of a brokerage site) or established fund managers. The fund manager spends the day investing and monitoring investments. When the trading day is over, shares of mutual funds are sold. In this sense, mutual funds are the opposite of ETFs. ETFs are actively traded on the stock market during the day from 9:30 am - 4 pm ET. You can buy or sell ETFs only during the day or you can queue a request overnight if you want to buy an ETF after trading hours have closed. Your request will be reviewed at 9:30 am and ready to trade.

- **ETFs have a lower cost**

By all statistics, ETFs cost less than Mutual Funds. The first reason an ETF is cheaper than a mutual fund is its passive nature. You may be in charge of your purchases, but you do not have to sit by and watch it all day. If you purchase an index like **QQQ**, you can simply sit back and watch things unfold. This makes it cheaper than hiring a fund manager. However, mutual funds, on average, would cost 0.7%, while ETFs costs 0.4%. With a standard observation, you'll notice that the more you buy, the lower your total cost is. If you are looking to invest long-term, buy and hold. People who buy and hold while investing long-term are playing a winners game.

- **ETFs are structurally passive**

By structure, you are not required to participate excessively in ETF funds. When purchasing an ETF, you have a small role to play unless you are looking to sell in the short-term. Since short-term investing is not the plan, you will likely remain passive while your ETF yields on its own. In the long-term, your strategy of buying and holding will continuously remain prosperous.

- **ETFs are not bounded by location**

This is a fact that no one seems to notice and is commonly overlooked. It is a surprising reality that mutual funds cannot be traded anywhere in the world. They can only be traded in their country of establishment. That is another subtle distinction between ETFs and Mutual Funds. ETFs can be bought and sold anywhere, as long as they are listed on the stock exchange market. I have friends in Europe who purchase ETFs on the US stock exchange market and have never stepped foot in the United States. How? All thanks to online brokerage platforms. Today, anyone who's anywhere in the world can invest, which makes the stock market stronger than ever. It may not sound like a big deal to a person living in the US, but for a person living somewhere other than the US, you might appreciate it more.

It is additionally apparent to mention that a person in the US can tap into foreign ETFs. For example, Nikkei **(NI225)** is an index on the Tokyo stock exchange.

- **Transparency and ease of access**

Transparency is a top tier feature of ETFs. All activities are open to the public and can be studied by all investors. Information can be easily accessed since most of its activities are tracked on the internet. You are directly in charge of your funds. You can observe the changes and prospects in your ETF yourself. You will not have to rely on a yearly report from a fund manager as it often happens in the mutual fund system. You can change up your ETF investment to your liking 24/7 with access to a computer.

- **Emphasis on index tracking**

On a large scale, ETFs pay more attention to index funds. They are often invested in index funds that auto-select their stocks. This is very good for a hands-off investor who wants to invest without the stress of constantly checking their portfolio. This implies that you do not have too many stocks to keep tabs on. An index would naturally make efforts to choose its best stocks and outperform its previous record. If your ETF tracks an index fund, you merely relax and casually observe its progress. Let AI do the work for you. As for mutual funds, we cannot be certain. A fund manager will undoubtedly tell you what kind of stocks he/she is putting your money into, but there is no guarantee they will be indexes.

- **Tax efficiency**

ETFs are better than mutual funds regarding taxes. ETFs generate low capital gains. They also have owner redemptions and portfolio turnover. All of these factors trim down the total tax they incur. Your tax is not evaded; it is just reduced.

The Types of ETFs

I am going to describe ETFs in two ways. First, according to how they are managed, and second, according to how they operate. It might sound like you are in a classroom, but you need to know these facts before setting out to invest in ETFs. Besides, being in a classroom to learn about money isn't such a bad idea. I wish they offered investment courses at my high school.

ETFs According to How They are Managed

- **Index-based funds**

I pointed out that ETFs are mostly passive. The primary reason behind its passive nature is because it takes the form of an index fund. You remember that index funds do not have to be keenly monitored. Index funds track a set of stocks that are automatically chosen as the best performers. As such, anyone investing in ETFs may worry less about monitoring their portfolio. This way, you don't have to feel stressed about managing your money. You can routinely invest and then forget about it. Let compound interest work its magic while you sit back and relax.

Gordon Scott even notes that the most notable ETFs are index stocks. At present (2020), no less than 1,200 index funds are tracked as an ETF. You surely remember Power-Shares **(QQQ)**. PowerShares is an ETF provider. Additionally, you can trade the S&P 500 Index as an ETF. It is tracked by SPDR S&P 500 ETF **(SPY)**.

- **Actively managed funds**

On the flip side, ETFs can be managed actively. This usually happens in a situation where the stocks bought by an ETF are not indexed. When you invest in an actively managed fund, you or your ETF adviser is keen on achieving an investment objective. As such, they may continually purchase a stock on your portfolio as much as they find necessary. The only problem with this class of stock is that it tilts towards striking an objective rather than fully tracking an index. This makes it unbalanced and challenging to follow.

Other Classifications

It is a bit surprising. There is an unusually broad range of ETF classifications. They could be classified according to the industry they track, the currency, the investment goal, the type of stocks (whether commodities or bonds), and many others. In a compact version, below are three classes of ETFs.

- **Stock ETF**

There are a variety of stocks on the market, and that is no news to you by now. Many of them are large-cap, for example, SPDR S&P 500 ETF, which tracks the S&P 500 in the version of an ETF. Some others are mid-size cap like iShares Russell 1000 ETF. In contrast, the Russell 2000 index is small-cap because the index compiles 2000 small size stocks. Depending on your investment objectives, you may invest in any ETF that tracks any of these indexes.

Similarly, stocks may vary according to the country they target. Most ETFs track the United States Stock Exchange Market, while a smaller number like, iShares MSCI EAFE ETF **(EFA)**, prefers to track international stocks that do not involve the United States.

One last thing. Stocks may also be grouped according to the sectors they track. PowerShares **(QQQ)**, which tracks non-financial companies, is a handy example of this. Several others track green power, financial institutions, agriculture, technology, healthcare, et cetera.

- **Bond ETF**

Similarly, you may choose an ETF that tracks bonds. You can directly invest in various bonds, and you may invest via bond mutual funds. A bond ETF is another medium through which you may invest in corporate bonds and treasury securities. It is passively managed, and it is not as popular as most other ETFs. Though, reports indicate that as of May 2020, up to 318 million dollars have been invested in ETF bonds.

Bond ETFs are not treasury security, so assets do not mature. Though, you are entitled to dividends, which are usually distributed monthly, outside the capital gains that may be distributed at the year-end. There is also a chance that your principal investment may have lost some value with a fluctuating economy. Nevertheless, you will get steady dividends. Bond ETFs offer low return and have low risk. When the market is bullish, stock ETFs are the best selection for an investor in their 20's.

- **Commodity ETF**

Commodity ETFs are among the costliest ETFs. They are traded as shares that track precious metals, hydrocarbons, agricultural products, and natural resources. More often than not, a commodity ETF tracks a single index, which means the fund is passively managed. At other times, it invests in future contracts.

As the record has proven, commodity ETFs offer a broad range of diversification. They often create a benchmark index. All of these factors imply that you can invest and maintain hands-off as a young, working investor. Tracking errors have occured when commodity ETF indexes clash with broader indexes that track a similar product.

This sounds complicated, but here is a simple breakdown. A commodity ETF tracks a gold company stock and combines it with a self-generated index. If the company is a large-cap company tracked by **QQQ**, there are chances the two could clash, and tracking errors might arise.

Silver and gold are leading examples. Over the Long-term, gold and silver only increase in value, like real-estate assets. Why you ask, inflation. You may invest in them through ETFs like **SLV** and **GLD**. Outside these two highly respectable commodity ETFs, I strongly recommend that you conduct thorough research. You should consider funda-mental and technical analysis.

Beyond the types of ETFs that have been extensively discussed, I have to remind you that there are several others. There are some others like currency ETFs, inverse ETFs, and so on. However, I did vouch from the beginning that I would show the most reliable, tried, and tested methods of invest-ments to guarantee you a steady future. All that said, there is one last thing to look into before purchasing an ETF.

Factors to Consider Before Selecting Your ETF

- **Cost**

The first and most important factor to be considered is your expense. You are in for business, and it's ideal to profit as much as possible. ETFs have impressive rates in compar-ison to mutual funds. To sample your cost and test your return, take the last year's earnings from a fund and subtract it by the fund's expense. This will show you the return on investment the fund provided the previous year. You can do this for the last five years because we all know that just because an ETF performed good or bad the past year does not mean it will duplicate identically next year.

- **Tracking rate**

Can you conveniently track your stocks? This is a question you must always be able to answer. One of the benefits ETFs offer over traditional mutual funds is the availability to track performance 24/7, rather than waiting until your fund manager updates you in six months or a year. If you own your own mutual fund without a manager, you can track the price of it in after hours. You want to be particularly sure that the tracking error rate of an ETF is minimal. If you research an ETF and find that it is hard to track or it has a high error rate, it may be a mistake to invest in those types of ETFs.

- **Diversification**

Diversification sounds like a great idea. We have earlier agreed that it mitigates your risks and expands your proba-bility of overall portfolio profit. However, diversification can become a problem with ETFs. It is rare, but you need to be sure that your preferred ETF does not over diversify, as that might make it too difficult to track. This usually happens when an ETF is constantly switching out companies for its index algorithm. Just a fair warning, it is nothing too serious to worry about. Furthermore, you want to guarantee that the ETF is not heavily constricted.

- **Liquidity**

Is liquidity still guaranteed? You should not take "maybe" or "no" for an answer. Another prominent advantage of an ETF is the ability to sell at anytime. If an ETF does not guarantee liquidity for any reason, you may want to reconsider your options.

Action To Take: Buy an ETF

Highly Respectable ETFs Include:

1. The Vanguard Total Stock Market ETF **(VTI)**
2. Schwab US Dividend Equity ETF **(SCHD)**
3. VanEck Vectors Gold Miners ETF **(GDX)**
4. Vanguard Value ETF **(VTV)**
5. iShares Dow Jones Select Dividend ETF **(DVY)**

ENDING THOUGHTS

We have discussed the structuring needed and the intentions of purchasing an ETF. If ETFs interest you, typically look for the ETFs with the lowest expense ratio. This strategy isn't only for ETFs. It is also for every stock you decide to purchase. The lower your expense ratio means the more money in your pocket. You will need to weigh out the possible return with the potential risk.

ETFs are confusing, I know. It has similarities to mutual funds, index funds, and more. The fact of the matter is becoming a successful investor doesn't necessarily mean understanding the entire marketplace. It is not essential to understand the whole market; try to understand the section of the market you choose to invest in. Early on in his investing career, Warren Buffett passed up an enormous offer by his friend Bill Gates. Gates wanted Buffett to invest significant capital into Microsoft before the stock was hot. Warren Buffett turned him down and decided to invest his extra cap space into chewing gum. That's right, Buffett turned down Microsoft for chewing gum. Although it may seem like a missed opportunity, Mr. Buffett describes the situation as beneficial. He says he didn't understand computers and would not invest in a business he did not understand. He was content investing in a business model he understood well. Warren Buffett was delighted to make money from the investments he understood so he wished Bill Gates the best of luck. Buffett illustrated a powerful lesson that day. Stick to what you're good at. This way, you can become an expert in the area of the market that matters to your success. Keep the main thing the main thing.

"It's a terrible mistake to think you have to have an opinion on everything. You only have to have an opinion on a few things. I don't worry to much about the things I don't understand."

— WARREN BUFFETT

I will explain the same concept using a different example. The length of the United States tax code is unknown. Some say there are over 60,000 pages of tax-related case law. There are very successful tax lawyers who don't understand a significant portion of the tax code. What these tax lawyers focus on are the most successful deductions they can achieve for their clients. Also known as saving their clients the most amount of money possible during tax time. Investing in the stock market isn't so different. As a successful investor, you don't have to memorize the intricate descriptions explaining Dividend-Paying Stocks, Index Funds, Mutual Funds, ETFs, REITs, or TIPS. Deeply understanding a few investments is more profitable than averagely understanding them all. Over time, confidently selecting the right investments for your financial goals become more comfortable. Give this information months and years to digest in your brain fully. If you are fond of continuous learning, you will want to continue being enriched with information about investing. There is one thing directly connected to long-term learning, long-term wealth building, and long-term success. It's time. And for someone in their 20's, we have a lot of time to learn and grow.

"You don't have to be right about thousands of companies, you only have to be right about a couple."

— WARREN BUFFETT

8

REAL ESTATE INVESTMENT TRUST (REIT)

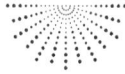

Real estate is one of the most sought out investments around the world. From the beginning of time, real estate holds so much value that power is sometimes affiliated with real estate ownership in some government systems. To many people, it is, in fact, the first form of stock they can think of.

"The best investment on earth is the earth itself."

— LOUIS GLICKMAN

If you are an avid fan of real estate, you're in luck. This chapter will discuss how you can get involved in real estate, not only from the physical side of buying property but, more importantly, Real Estate Investment Trusts (REITs). This chapter will discuss the best way to get involved in real estate stocks. First, let's discuss some history.

Millions of people try to invest in real estate. More often than not, the real estate they invest in is a property that houses themselves and their family. Owning property to house your family is the first priority, but do you have the ambition to own other forms of property? Realty Shares carried out a 2017 study that revealed that around 20% of Americans are interested in owning assets they could lease or sell in the future. This is not news, really. Andrew Carnegie once declared that ninety percent of all millionaires in America had been made through real estate.

People are enthusiastic about real estate. If there is a stock on the market that deals in real estate, it certainly has prospects for investors who want to jump in. Thankfully for investors, there are Real Estate Investment Trusts (REITs).

What's great about REITs? By law, 90% of the income made from a REIT gets distributed to shareholders in the form of dividends. REITs invest in almost every kind of real estate you can think of, including others you wouldn't think of.

Let's first begin with the question, **how is Real Estate defined?**

Real estate is landed property. It is a piece of land you own, and you have the right to build whatever you want on it.

"Real estate is property made up of land and the buildings on it, as well as the natural resources of the land, including uncultivated flora and fauna, farmed crops and livestock, water, and any additional mineral deposits."

— JAMES CHEN

Your land, and whatever you place on it, is real estate property. Real estate can be an office, a farm, a shopping mall, an apartment complex, or an ordinary piece of land.

Nonetheless, there is a line of distinction you should note. Real estate should not be confused with personal wealth. Personal wealth is a byproduct of owning real estate.

Let's answer the next big question. **How do you invest in real estate?**

Go down the street and ask anyone. You should be unsurprised to discover that despite their financial complications, every human out there wants to have a home. We all want a cozy place to get away from the weather, lay our heads, and raise our families. It is undoubtedly not an awkward request. For anyone without a home to live in, they will continue to struggle towards getting that comfort.

- **Residential real estate**

Residential real estate is when a person decides to lease out a home they have purchased. You might buy a property in a remote location and rent it out to a few tenants. It could be a townhouse, an undeveloped property, a condominium, as long as it is resident-oriented, it is considered residential real estate. As the owner, you are paid weekly, monthly, or annually, depending on the contract you agree on with your tenants. Buying real estate has been associated with the American dream for generations.

- **Commercial real estate**

Commercial real estate is relatively similar to residential real estate. The primary difference is commercial real estate focuses on building for official purposes. Commercial real estate specializes in warehouses, stores, offices, and similar settings. These real estates typically yield more ROI because there is more money and more risk at stake. Since people often require offices, warehouses, and company sites, the return on investment is substantial, especially over the long-term. Sounds good, but it's difficult to get into commercial real estate because of two barriers.

Certification to lease commercially and a large
sum of money to get in the door

Many of us in our 20's don't have either. So, how can we get involved and profit from a dependable money making industry?

After a brief lesson on the history and types of real estate investments, we will uncover the number one way you can effortlessly make money from the real estate business.

Analysis Behind the Federal Reserve Bank of St. Louis

Real estate investors know that regardless of the cost, people do everything they can to have a home. The Federal Reserve Bank of St. Louis records that there has been a steady increase in the price of homes in the United States, officially starting in 1963. You can see the up-roaring trend in the chart below:

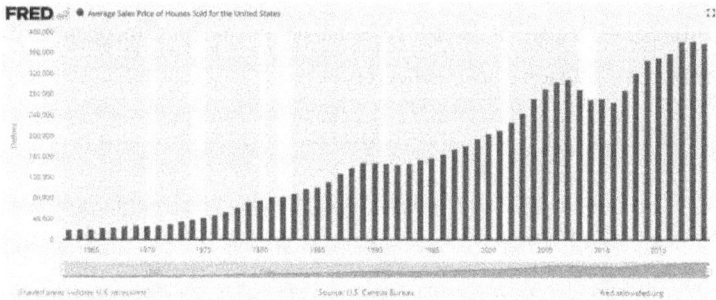

Source: Federal Reserve Bank of St. Louis.

As you can see from the graph, the price of homes continue to rise with creeping inflation rates. It sparks my curiosity why the recession of 2008 did not have a lasting negative effect on the price of real estate. We can attribute the record high prices to the common phrase, *bad times never last*. If you buy low, the market will come up, and you can sell high. The price of homes are higher now than ever recorded.

As a young and inexperienced entrepreneur, I believed becoming a landlord was the only way to make money from real estate. I was under the assumption that the only way to make money from real estate was to save up tens of thousands of dollars, buy a residential home, and rent it out. Interestingly, this is not the case. Landlords who own homes, uncultivated land, or stores are not the only type of real estate investors. There are at least five types of real estate investments, and we will talk about them now.

Five Types of Real Estate Investments

- **Rentals**

Rental properties are the most common type of real estate investment. It is the type of investment where you are a property owner and caretaker.

> *"Everyone wants a piece of land. It's the only sure investment. It can never depreciate like a car or washing machine. Land will only double its value in ten years."*
>
> — SAM SHEPARD

Investing in rental properties imply that you own residential homes, stores, condos, uncultivated land, vacation homes, et cetera that can be leased out to people for a fixed period. Owning the asset is not your only responsibility. Additionally, you are actively in charge of their operations, use, and management.

On the surface, becoming a landlord would sound like a picnic job. You are the landlord, and you can tell anyone exactly what you want or do not want on your property. You are also receiving steady income rent from your property(ies). It certainly doesn't seem difficult. However, an interview with a popular real estate investor, Joshua Kennon, revealed that this is not the case. Becoming a landlord can be a draining job.

As a property manager, it is important to vet potential home renters before you decide to enter into a contract with them. Something that is often overlooked when buying a rental property is the potential of getting dragged to court by your tenants. Or dragging one of your tenants to court for a misdemeanor. No one dreams of waking up to discover that all of their life's efforts have been wasted because of negligent tenants. It requires a lot of knowledge from zoning regulations to executive decisions.

Strangely, this is the type of real estate investment that most people opt for, especially when they head towards retirement. They usually become full-time caretakers of their real estate assets. In cases where the landlord hires real estate managers, they often report ridiculously high profit rates. This is a more advanced real estate management approach because it takes a relatively large sum of money and resources. Buying up properties then hiring someone to manage those properties is a high stake investment. Nevertheless, it is proven to be profitable by all statistics.

- **Flipping**

Flipping is the second most popular type of real estate investment. It is common among business people who desire to reserve their funds for a brief period. It is fast becoming a substitute for investing in the stock market. This is probably because it can yield a high return in a short period of time.

"Land is land, and it is safer than the stocks and bonds of Wall Street Swindlers."

— EUGENE O'NEILL

New real estate investors tend to flip property because it gives an immediate flow of profit right back into their pockets. In response, this provides the investor with more cash they can reinvest back into their real estate business. Investors will also use this money to diversify their stock portfolio so that if the housing market crashes, they have a backup source of income.

Okay, but how exactly does flipping work?

Flipping real estate is buying properties and holding them for a period, after which they are sold at profitable margins. The flip investor would usually hold the property for as little time as possible, except in cases with long-term potential. Admittedly, there are always long-term prospects. You will agree that long-term prospects have their benefits if you go by the diagram illustrated by the Federal Reserve Bank of St. Louis chart.

John Jacob perfectly describes real estate flipping when he advises that you should,

---

"Buy on the fringe and wait. Buy land near a growing city! Buy real estate when other people want to sell. Hold what you buy."

— JOHN JACOB

There are Two Types of Flipping

1. Face-lift style

This is when an investor purchases a property from a seller then fixes the property up in a more presentable form. Usually, properties like these are bought in terrible shape, then upgraded at an inexpensive cost. After the remodeling phase, the property returns to the market and is sold at a higher price than the initial cost + improvement costs. In turn, face-lift style investors achieve a profitable margin.

2. Hold and resell

Hold and resell is not so different from the previous style. The main difference is that you buy when people want to sell, as John Jacob advises, and hold it until real estate is valued higher in your area. Though, you run the risk of legal cases, government intrusion, and so on. Worst, you may never sell that property at a satisfactory amount. This style of flipping is dependent on the market value of the surrounding properties rising in value. It is best to hold and resell when purchasing a property in a new and growing city.

- **REIG**

Real Estate Investment Group (REIG) is the third class of real estate investments. It exists in a situation where multiple people combine their funds and establish a partnership agreement. A group of people or REIG companies invest in real estate properties and share the cost and profit. It's similar to mutual funds but with tangible property.

Here is how it works. A real estate company is set up by a real estate manager(s). This company then conducts some extensive research and buys promising properties. Then, investors are invited to purchase stake in the company. Through this medium, an individual investor may own a portion of the real estate property without managing it themselves. The portion they own will be determined by the percentage of their contribution to the project. The ROI from rents is also shared according to the percentage of each member's stake.

Clearly, it is similar to mutual funds where you deposit your funds, and you are hands-off, expecting yields. Your real estate manager would take some percentage as commission from your gain too. Some REIGs are dissolved after a few months, while some continue to function as fully established companies. Usually, investing can be done in the stock market, but REIG companies prefer not to enlist.

- **Property crowdfunding**

Crowdfunding is one of the newest forms of investing in the real estate market. Fundraising and investments are made on a crowdfunding platform. A crowdfunding platform is a channel designed to generate funds for an entrepreneur or a group of entrepreneurs. People who have business ideas and do not have the funds required may table their thoughts on a crowdfunding platform. Interested investors appear, invest, and own shares or stake according to their investment amount. Crowdfunding platforms are hosted as a website, social media outlet, et cetera.

In this case, a real estate company is able to generate a large sum of funds to complete a project. The profits from the project are then distributed to you, the investor. The company responsible for the real estate contract dispense profits to investors according to their investment quota.

This is great for investors who want to own a piece of the pie but take a hands-off approach. All you need is a computer and the internet.

Ideally, the investor sends money through a crowdfunding platform and receives passive income that exceeds their initial investment. Real estate investments online are simple. If this interests you, below are five respected and credible platforms you can check out.

- CrowdStreet
- Fundrise
- DiversyFund
- EquityMultiple
- RealtyMogul

CrowdStreet, for example, has a minimum investment of $25,000. Although that seems steep and intimidating, other platforms don't require as high of a minimum. DiversyFund, for example, has a minimum investment of $500 with a 0% fee. Including an average annual return of 11% to 18% depending on the investment. There are pros and cons to each platform, so doing your own research is necessary before investing.

Crowdfunding platforms are a fantastic way for real estate investors to make some steady income and add an appealing type of investment to their entire portfolio of investments.

- **REIT**

Real Estate Investment Trusts (REITs) are a thrilling way to invest in real estate. This is the most explosive real estate investment sold on the stock market. 90% of profits are distributed to shareholders in the form of dividends. Any stock that pays good dividends while simultaneously holding the stock long-term allows compound interest to make you tons of money. So, How do REITs work?

A Real Estate Investment Trust is a commercial real estate company. It is usually set up as a large corporation that deals in all sorts of real estate properties, from uncultivated land to entirely built offices, shopping centers, hotels, malls, and hospitals. I don't want you to be misinformed, Real Estate Investment Trust (REIT) is not notably different from a Real Estate Investment Group (REIG). The principles are almost identical besides one key difference. REITs are traded on the stock market, and REIGs are not.

Structurally, a REIT is large enough to be traded on the stock market. A foremost real estate researcher, Mark Cussen, once mentioned that REITs used to be traded in the market as subsets in the energy investment sector. Things remained that way until the Global Industry Classification Standard (GICS) considered it a different set of assets and adjusted the rules.

Now, REIT is considered a distinct asset on the stock market and traded like every other stock. You can invest in REIT shares, which means you will own a stake in real estate properties without directly getting involved. It is also known to yield more profits than most other stocks on the market due to their impressive dividends. However, there can be complications. The first is that investors are hardly handy in the market. As such, it might be difficult to sell or buy REIT shares. Some REIT shares are publicly traded while others are not. With trading platforms like Robinhood, who buy and sell REITs with high levels of liquidity, you won't run into a problem when trading REITs.

In cases where a REIT diversifies beyond real estate properties, it usually maintains a minimum of 70% investment in real estate. This way, REITs often remain grounded in the pursuit of real estate properties. If you have ever aspired to invest in real estate properties, REIT might be a handy solution. REIT shares are not as volatile as growth stocks. Many REITs are very reliable, and there are rarely surprises. There are three methods of trading REITs, and we'd better see about them now.

3 Types of REITs

- **Equity REITs**

Equity REITs specialize in rents and sales. They generate income from rents paid by tenants, and they often offer a high dividend. Also, they generate profit from capital gains made from the sale of properties. They are less risky than the others, and they might be just for you if you are not in the market for high risk and high reward.

- **Mortgage REITs**

Next in line, mortgage REITs direct all of their attention to mortgage investments. What makes mortgage REITs different from equity REITs is that they specialize in mortgage services. They are directly into sales, and they generate a higher profit. The only point in question is that mortgage REITs are riskier. They are prone to higher debts than most other types of investments. Debtors may run into financial complications, file bankruptcy, and become unable to pay their debts. If this were 2007, you would not want to buy shares of mortgage REITs because your shares would have drastically crashed in 2008 due to the mortgage crisis. A disaster like the crash in 2008 would lead to a significant drop in the value of assets and shares. If you are an audacious risk-taker, this is just for you. When the mortgage business is going smoothly, mortgage REITs are a great option: high risk, high reward.

- **Hybrid REITs**

Hybrid REITs are the umbrella form of real estate investments. It covers all the necessary types of investments provided by the two options earlier mentioned, in no particular order. A hybrid REIT determines the trend from the market and selects the best options at the moment. Due to its diversity, it presents fewer risks too.

After discussing the types of REITs, let's discuss how you can purchase shares.

In general, there are three ways to invest in REITs.

Various Methods of Trading

- **Publicly traded REITs**

Publicly traded REITs are the most popular and accessible type of REIT. There are large REIT corporations that are listed on every major stock exchange in the United States. Many publicly-traded REITs are traded on the NASDAQ and NYSE markets. They operate on the same regulatory measures as other stocks. If you'd like to check out some, Simon Property Group (which is traded on NYSE as **SPG**) is an example. Self-Storage REIT (NYSE: **PSA**) is another example.

Side note: When looking at any two companies side by side, a common question I get is, "which one is better"? An investor who has done their research can make prosperous claims for both companies. The hard truth is that you, as an investor, need to do your own research. Take research from this book when weighing whether a stock is bullish or bearish. Most experts use information online to make their picks while others use a self-made formula when picking stocks. There are no right answers to picking that magical stock that will give you explosive earnings day in and day out. No one on earth has 20/20 pilot vision to pick the best stock at the best time. Many people aspire to find the secret to see through a magic ball that will tell them the absolute right answer. Often, we find that our magic ball too cloudy for us to make the best decision. The trick is to self educate yourself in order to remove some of the fog and see a little better into the theoretical magic ball. Knowing what to look for has been a key instrument throughout this book. When you know what to look for, the objective of picking the right stocks become easier.

- **Publicly non-listed REITs**

Another option is publicly non-listed REITs. You may purchase their shares and become an active shareholder.

However, you would not find their stocks on any major exchange. This is because they are not enlisted on the stock market. You will have to consider other media platforms when investing in such companies. You should also understand that publicly non-listed companies are not bounded as REITs, they might offer varying features, especially in dividend sharing, liquidity, and volatility.

What I am pointing out is that you should expect them to offer different methods of dividend sharing. You should also note their liquidity rate differs because their stocks are not usually liquid. Nevertheless, you are as protected as you would be if you were opting for a listed REIT. A handy example is a Real Estate Investment Group, where investors purchase shares and hold stake in the company without venturing into the stock market. Crowdfunding is another example. Ways to become involved were detailed in the previous pages.

- **Private REITs**

Lastly, private REITs are exclusive types of REITs that are not open to the public. An investor would still own shares, but the only difference is that you can't find shares to buy on the market. They are sold and managed by brokers. You'd have to meet specific requirements. Such conditions may include a minimum amount of investment, a minimum annual income, et cetera. The individuals who meet such categories are considered "accredited investors." Investing in private REITs take more paperwork, persistence, and resources.

While private REITs are not so popular because of extra demands, they have yielded more profits than most other investments. This makes sense though. An exclusive and private REIT is more difficult to participate in because these REITSs are for *big fish investors*. It is difficult to get involved in private REITs because to qualify, a sufficient amount of funds is required on retainer. Most 20-year-olds do not have that amount of cash floating around.

Benefits of REIT Investments

Most of us in our 20's will shoot for publicly traded hybrid REITs. As stated in previous sections, these REITs offer a mix of real estate diversity and are easily accessible to the common investor.

- **High dividend yields**

From all appearances, REITs yield a higher dividend than most other companies in the stock market. To re-enforce the major reason why REITs are one of the 7 investments chosen is REITs are mandated to distribute a minimum of 90% of its profits to investors. If the company running the REIT makes money, so do you. As strange as it sounds, records show REITs have been more profitable than the S&P 500 Index. This trend may continue since the real estate industry continues to boom in many US cities.

Because REITs have been more profitable than the S&P 500, it does not mean you should put all of your eggs into one basket. REITs or any other investment detailed throughout this book is not intended as the only way to build long-term wealth. The investments detailed throughout are intended to be combined together as a way of encapsulating financial stability. Spreading your funds between 5, 10, or 15 long-term investment options will ensure your portfolio is well rounded and prepared for a downturn in the market.

- **Steady capital yields**

REITs tend to guarantee a steady capital yield. If you have just invested in a REIT with landed properties, for instance, the price of the land might soar in only a few years. This means that you are earning dividends as a shareholder. Simultaneously, your capital has increased in value since the land will probably be sold at a price higher than the initial cost (land tends to go up in value). This is not all. The land may be developed and sold or rented at a higher rate. These factors point to the fact that REITs can generate a steady rise in capital for years to come.

- **Diversification**

As you might have noted, diversification is key to security in investments. There are ups and downs in every investment, and surprises will spring. The only way to mitigate losses from such a situation is to diversify your investments. Regardless of the REIT type you venture into, you are guaranteed diversification over the entire stock market.

As an illustration, an equity REIT may engage in land, hotel, residence, and office rents. Normally, you would be unable to participate in all of these divisions as a person who hasn't gone to school to get a licensed certification. Since the REIT covers all the decisions for you, your funds will be spread across most real estate sectors, and you are secured against downtrend in any of the individual real estate divisions.

- **Liquidity**

To some extent, REIT shares are also considered liquid. They can be easily bought and dispensed for cash, mainly if you are trading on a listed and publicly traded REIT. If you are considering the others, it might get a little tricky. Nevertheless, you should have no trouble if you are consulting a broker.

- **REITs have no corporate tax**

Much to your benefit as a real estate investor, REITs are relieved of corporate tax (subject to change depending on the presidential administration). The regulation demands that REITs dispense up to 90% of its income as dividends to shareholders. That implies that raising your dividends is a priority for established REIT companies. This makes it all the more ideal for a long-term investment.

- **Hedge against inflation**

Real estate can not be destroyed by inflation. In fact, the value of every property rises with general inflation. Theoretically, investing in a REIT implies that you have reserved the value of your funds against inflation at any point.

3 Facts that You Should Remember When Investing in REIT

- **One size does not fit all**

This is not an S&P 500 or Nasdaq-100 index fund. It would be best to remember that the type of REIT you invest in will specialize in offices, residential homes, healthcare facilities, shopping malls, hotels or many other types of grounded real estate. The value placed on each of these can determine how much your total yield will be. Usually, offices would charge higher than residential spaces. Offices require a lot of funds for maintenance too. You will need to learn these dynamics and consider your preference before investing in a variety of REITs.

- **Dividend taxation**

As I have earlier pointed out, a REIT skips taxation as long as the company distributes a minimum of 90% of its profits back to investors. But that is not where it ends. An individual dividend is taxed the same way as personal income is taxed. You will be taxed on your dividends earned by the federal government as income tax. With any investment, take time to consider yields, taxes, and sector specifics before selecting a REIT.

- **Staying in the safe zone**

Everyone likes to be guaranteed security and peace of mind. We want to be sure that our hard-earned money will continuously grow in the marketplace regardless of what happens. Nevertheless, you have to bear in mind that investing involves risk: the higher your risk, the higher your reward. You should overcome the fear that a stock seems too risky to invest. If it holds enough prospects in the long-term future, shoot at it. Use your judgment when making decisions. *No one cares more about your money than you.*

Action To Take: Buy an REIT

Highly Respectable REITs Include:

1. Preferred Apartment Communities **(APTS)**
2. Equinix **(EQIX)**
3. iShares Core US REIT ETF **(USRT)**
4. Vanguard US REIT fund **(VNQ)**
5. SPDR Dow Jones REIT ETF **(RWR)**

ENDING THOUGHTS

History has shown that the value of the paper dollar decreases year after year. On average, without a 3% raise each year, our standard of living decreases due to inflation. I don't have to tell you that this is concerning. As previously observed, real estate investing is one of the best ways to protect your money against inflation. REITs pay high dividends, build property in growing cities, and provide long-term security when re-investing dividend payments. Preferred Apartment Communities **(APTS)**, for example, currently pay a dividend yield of 15.85. Any dividend yield above 5.0 makes an investor exited to research the inner working of the company and see if that investment is right for him/her. Typically, REITs don't drastically increase or decrease their share price like growth stocks but with a high dividend rate investors do not need to see the stock price soar. On the other hand, Equinix **(EQIX)** REIT is up 203% in the past 5 years. This is a REIT that has a lower dividend yield but has a high growth in stock price. Re-investing those monthly, quarterly, or yearly dividends compound into miraculous figures. REITs are easy to trade on brokerage sites like Fidelity, E-trade, Robinhood, and many more.

Here and now, I am tempted to ask you, have you added another investment to your list?

9

TREASURY INFLATION-PROTECTED SECURITIES (TIPS)

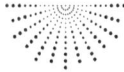

H ave you heard anything about Treasury Securities? We earlier agreed that we would not consider myths, fables, or old stories. We will dive straight into details right here and nowhere else. So, what are Treasury Inflation-Protected Securities, and why do I think you might consider it as a long-term investment?

In the first place, what are Treasury Securities? Kimberly Amadeo is a stock market analyst who's work I thoroughly enjoy. To use her words,

---

"A Treasury Security is a bond issued out to the public by the United States Government. It is one of the steady things you can touch in the stock market."

— KIMBERLY AMADEO

In practical terms, treasury securities are one of the

government's ways of sourcing funds to run its administration. It would be best if you were not surprised; the government usually finds it impractical to run every state on taxpayer dollars alone. Shout out to my high school economics class for peaking my interest in treasury securities. Anyway, there are national and international investments. Many treasury securities do not yield until an extended period has been reached. The United States government sells securities to citizens who hold their security for a number of years then are reimbursed for a profit. In short, investors lend the government their money in expectation of a greater ROI in the future. First, they are auctioned on the Federal Trade Reserve Bank of New York. Then, they are subsequently traded on secondary markets for outsider people like you and I to trade.

The securities sold to the public are fixed for a period that may span between a year to thirty years (in the United States). The period of maturity is determined by the type of security you opt for. As one would expect, the government makes all efforts to raise funds within legal means. The United States government has been paying treasury securities sense 1929. The instant your security is due, you will be paid in full.

Over and above that, you should know that there are different types of treasury securities. After we discuss their types in full, I will share with you my preferred choice. I will keep the first two options to the point until I discuss the significant investment that excites. You will enjoy it, no doubt.

The Types of Treasury Securities

- **Treasury bills**

Treasury bills are the simplest version of treasury securities. Dr. Natalie Boyd discusses them extensively in a speech. She points out that treasury bills are bills you buy before their maturity date. A maturity date is a future date when a bond will be worth a higher amount than what you paid for it. Dr. Boyd also points out that treasury bills can be bought in denominations of $1000.

Let's get practical. In a situation where you are buying a treasury bill, you pay a discount less than the bill's value. Your target bill might be worth $1000, for example, you could pay $900. The current Consumer Price Index determines the amount you pay. You pay the $900 now, and then on your maturity date, you turn in your bill for $1000. You are paid the full amount of your matured $1000 treasury bill. This type of investment is short-term only. Your bill may mature in a week or in a few months. However, you are guaranteed its maturity within a year. For clarity, you may purchase as many treasury bills as you would like (maximum denomination is $5 million). At the end of the specified time, your bill matures to its full amount. In turn, making you, the investor, a small profit.

- **Treasury notes**

A treasury note is vastly different from a treasury bill. The striking difference between a T-Bill and a T-Note is that a treasury bill attracts a fixed percentage while a treasury note attracts interest. Both are issued by the US government under a treasury security.

Ideally, a treasury note matures in about two to ten years.

It also pays a fixed interest rate that is distributed every six months. Although, take note that the interest distributed does not compound. In some cases, a treasury note can adjust its interest rate quarterly. A note like that is called a Floating Rate Note.

To obtain a treasury note, you pay the full amount and receive your interest every six months. By way of illustration, you may choose to obtain a $3000 Treasury Note. You will be required to pay $3000 in full. The interest paid on a Treasury Note is low by many standards. For a Five-Year Treasury Constant Maturity, the interest rate is 0.27% (August 2020). This is very low compared to the current bullish stock market. Regardless, interest will be paid every six months. If your treasury note matures in five years, you would have received $81 interest in five years. This is the sum of a 0.27% yield on a $3000 investment paid every six months. At the end of the fifth year, you are paid the $3000 you invested on day one and get to keep all the interest you occurred.

- **Treasury bonds**

Treasury bonds are another type of treasury security. They are structurally similar to treasury notes. They attract interest and offer a comparable interest rate every six months. The interest rate is fixed too. The interest paid out to investors does not compound. The only difference between a treasury note and a treasury bond lies in their time period. Treasury bonds may extend to thirty years, while a treasury note would mature in a maximum of ten years.

Before we get into the next section, I need to emphasize

that treasury securities as a whole is not an excellent way to make money. Why would I recommend an investment that doesn't make money? One reason, and I will give you a hint. It's in the name. *Security*. Treasury securities are the type of investment you want at the very bottom of your stock portfolio. When allocating your assets (deciding how much money you want to put in each investment), I wouldn't recommend investing any more than 5% of your funds into any treasury security. The idea here is to purchase a highly liquid ETF that will hold your excess funds in place of a traditional bank account. You can even think of this investment as an emergency fund in case disaster strikes unexpectedly in your life. A highly liquid ETF will give you very low returns but it gives security knowing you have access to your funds at anytime and it pays more interest than a traditional bank account.

The risk is so minimal that you can be confident storing a small amount of cash as a reserve fund. An ETF worth researching is iShares Core US Aggregate Bond ETF **(AGG)**. This ETF tracks inverse bonds. If you invest in **AGG** and the bond interest rate goes down, you make money. You are betting against the government bond interest rate. The more debt a country occurs, the lower their bond interest becomes. Why? Governments don't like to increase the interest they pay on loans if they are struggling to pay back government debt. Theoretically, as the years continue, the United States will continuously acquire more debt (US national debt has risen consistently from 1981 - present). In turn, lowering the US bond interest rate. Cause and effect, AGG stock price goes up. In the short-term this varies a few points, but it is common sense investing when looking long-term. The bond interest rate of the US government fluctuates yearly due the current administration and economic issues. Over the long-term (10-20 years) a stock like **AGG** is almost guaranteed to increase in stock value. In addition, paying a 2.29 dividend yield currently.

For the final time, I will reiterate that treasury securities are not an excellent investment to make money. It might be the right decision for the investor who wants a safe ETF they can store a fraction of their funds in as an emergency fund.

You now know that I do not recommend treasury bills, notes, or bonds in the fashion of making money. I only added these investment options into this book because of Warren Buffett's first rule. *"Rule No. 1: Never lose money."* We have already discussed the meaning behind this rule in an earlier section. Treasury bills, notes, and bonds are a way of conservatively protecting your money. Usually, investors purposely use this type of investment as a safety net.

I have chosen to recommend Treasury Inflation Protection Securities instead. You should not be taken by surprise, however. It will become more apparent in the next few paragraphs.

- **Treasury inflation protection securities (TIPS)**

Down to business, Treasury Inflation Protection Securities are the best type of securities for young men and women. They are not only ideal for long-term wealth; they also offer unrivaled security. Though, you should never invest all of your funds in a treasury security because it's used just for security. Why? TIPS should be used as a backend protection plan in your portfolio rather than dumping all your funds into TIPS as a front runner. The purpose of TIPS is to ensure your financial wealth, even if other sectors in your investment portfolio take a dip. The United States will pay its securities, no questions about that. The puzzling reality is that the interest rate is too low for TIPS to be your only long-term investment. As previously stated under the *treasury bills* section, there is little rhyme or reason to invest more than 5% of your total assets in a treasury security.

> **Securities should only be considered as a diversification tool in your investment portfolio.**

To the point, TIPS is an entirely different type of treasury bill.

"Indexed to inflation to protect investors from a decline in the purchasing power of money."

— JAMES CHEN

Complex? Okay. James Chen implies that TIPS are designed to protect an investor from inflation so their purchasing power does not diminish.

Take a minute and think about the value of money over time. Let's take the past thirty years for example. Imagine you invested $1000 30 years ago into TIPS.

You have invested your $1000 and done nothing with it. You will continue to get your interest every six month and you will receive your total payment at the end of thirty years. The cumulative rate of inflation was 98.2% from 1990 through 2020. Investing $1000 in 1990 would theoretically turn into $1,982.41 in 2020. I say theoretically because of two disputable principals.

1. *TIPS are not guaranteed investments*
2. *Prices can fluctuate*

Simplification of Benefits

1. Because TIPS are treasury bonds backed by the US government, TIPS are a low-risk investment.

2. Your money follows the trend of inflation, which historically, has risen every single year from 1955 to present.

Simplification of Risks

1. Tendency of short-term price fluctuation. Market prices significantly shift with changes to real interest rates. Meaning, the share price varies substantially over the short-term

2. Deflation. Over a long period of deflation a fund tracking TIPS will drop its share price.

Why Should You Consider TIPS?

Eric Petroff points out that TIPS are not entirely different from any other type of treasury security. What marks them apart is the introduction of the Consumer Price Index (CPI). CPI is a method of measuring changes in the essential cost of living. It is used to average the cost of medical expenses, transportation, and consumer goods, among others. It notes the rise or fall in the price of these basic necessities and adds or subtracts inflation or deflation from its deductions. Your investment will be raised to its equivalent CPI rate.

Let's uncover another example to simplify TIPS. The following example is conceptual (not intended to report a factual investment in TIPS). Let's say you invested $11,900 in TIPS in 1960. In 1960, the median home value was $11,900. At the end of your 10-30 years, you would receive the amount it would cost to buy that "same house" in the future year. So let's say you kept that $11,900 investment in TIPS for 30 years. Because TIPS track the Consumer Price Index, your initial investment of $11,900 in 1960 would turn into approximately $79,100 in 1990 (medium home value).

Now, as great as an example that was, it does have some flaws. TIPS are attached to the Consumer Price Index, not Real Estate value. When using an inflation calculator, $11,900 in 1960 would be equal to $52,544.93 in 1990. You'll notice that this evaluation is over $20,000 less than the purchasing of a house example. The reason why? There is not a definitive calculation because TIPS are not a guaranteed investment. Although TIPS are indexed to inflation, the current value is not guaranteed to increase during inflationary periods. The expectations of investors also affect the value of TIPS. You would think that the ratio would strictly follow the movements of inflation, but investor hype still plays a part in determining the stock price.

Having said that, the philosophy behind TIPS is brilliant. A fund that tracks inflation is useful for investors. Especially since inflation has risen for the past 65 years in a row! This is arguably why Treasury Inflation-Protected Securities are the best type of security.

So, here are the top reasons you should consider a Treasury Inflation-Protected Security:

- **Money is protected against inflation**

Inflation is the leading factor that devalues currency around the world. Inflation takes over the market and reduces currency value; by implication, a particular amount can no longer afford what it could earlier. In the absence of the gold standard, however, there is no way to protect long-term savings from a devaluation of paper dollars through inflation.

- **Principal stands to increase over time**

Unlike most other types of investments, TIPS can guarantee your principal will increase over time as long as the United States inflation increases. You do not have to increase your initial investment or do anything. As previously stated, your principal typically rises in proportion to the rate of inflation in the economy. This means if the CPI reports a 10% increase in the general cost of essential goods and services, your TIPS account should increase by 10%.

Let us consider an illustration for clarity. You invest $8000 in a fund tracking TIPS that matures in ten years. You will continue to receive dividends bi-annually at a fixed interest rate. Presumably, 2% every six months. If a 10% inflation occurs in any of these years, your principal would be upgraded by 10%. This means you would be deemed to have invested $8,800 from the start. Through this, the government ensures that your penny is worth more in the long-term.

- **Interest tends to increase**

Not only does your principal rise with inflation, but your interest increases too. In the United States, your principal is backed with a fixed interest rate. For example, you might be guaranteed a fixed interest rate of 1.5% every six months.

The discomforting snag is that the interest rate is usually low. Although, compared to other securities, it is more economical. You might be offered a ridiculous rate of 0.85-2%. Nevertheless, you should not be bothered.

High inflation is a continuous trend in our world. The prices of things keep soaring, and that will affect both your principal and your interest rates. Let's agree you invested $8000 over ten years again. A 10% inflation happened, and the face value of your principal expanded to $8,800. Naturally, your 2% will be upgraded in accordance with your new principal too. It used to be $160 every six months, and now, it is $176 every six months. Thank you compound interest! It will remain at this point until there is another shift in the economic value of the currency. That is a big plus.

Weaknesses of TIPS investment

Now with every pro, there is usually a con. If there wasn't pros and cons to every investment, everyone in the world would be investing in the same thing. Here is the list of cons for Treasury Inflation-Protection Securities.

- **Higher tax rate**

The first disheartening fact about TIPS is higher taxes. Generally, securities are not charged by local or state authorities in the United States. However, the Federal Government taxes the interest generated by securities. Since there is a chance that your profits will increase, your tax rate will proportionally rise with it.

- **Deflation might happen**

Inflation is not the only economic condition that can affect TIPS. Deflation is a condition that will decrease your holdings. Since your funds rise when inflation happens, it falls when deflation occurs too. With the current market, it looks highly unlikely for deflation to occur. The Great Recession in 2008 was devastating to the US economy but inflation still rose 0.1% that year.

- **Lower interest rate**

As a long-term investor, you want guarantees that your money will grow in leaps and bounds after investing for a period as long as 10-30 years. If you are interested in expanding, you'll need higher risk investments. TIPS interest rate is low compared to many other investment options detailed through this book. TIPS is fine for a backend cushion, not for the majority of your funds.

- **Not ideal in a stable economy**

One last weakness, this system is not ideal in a stable economy. You are guaranteed a lot of profit only when inflation happens and the country booms. A stable economy that doesn't move may not be so different from dumping the cash in a bank account, which we have ruled out from day one. TIPS is not advantageous when the economy is stagnant or in a deflationary period. To say the least, TIPS is way better than a bank account when compared side by side due to the United States record of continuous inflation.

How to Invest in TIPS

All that said, security and protection against inflation are enough reasons to consider investing in TIPS. If you are pinning it to your list, here is how to invest.

You may purchase individual bonds directly from the United States Treasury. This is usually cheaper, but you should know that you are stuck to only a few options.

You may also purchase bonds through brokers. This is usually costlier than purchasing individual bonds. The only plus is that it guarantees diversification. It invests in TIPS that mature at various times and offers multiple interest rates. You may not have access to all of these on your own.

The most common way to invest in TIPS are through the United States Stock Market. You can find TIPS through brokerage sites like Fidelity, Robinhood, E-trade and many more. Most of the TIPS on the stock exchange market are tracked by an ETF.

Action To Take: Buy TIPS

Highly Respectable TIPS Include:

1. Goldman Sachs Access Inflation Protected USD Bond ETF **(GTIP)**
2. iShares TIPS Bond ETF **(TIP)**
3. Schwab US TIPS ETF **(SCHP)**
4. Vanguard Short-Term Inflation-Protected Securities ETF **(VTIP)**
5. SPDR Portfolio TIPS ETF **(SPIP)**

ENDING THOUGHTS

Treasury Inflation-Protected Securities are the final investment. While REITs are the icing on the cake, TIPS are the cherry on top. What I am trying to say with this absurd reference is that like a cherry on top of a cake, TIPS are not a necessity. TIPS add extra flavor to your investment portfolio if you are truly dedicated to invest for 20+ years. The five examples listed above are among the most sought after TIPS stocks but you will notice that the stock price doesn't move much. The five stocks above, averaged 11% for the past 5 years and paying a low dividend yield of about 1.1-1.83. It is extremely rare for TIPS to ever head in a downward trend that is why it is one of the most secure set of stocks on the stock exchange market. When investing, you won't see a high rise in stock price but that is not the purpose for owning TIPS. I recommend using TIPS as your cash reserve. Think of it as your stock portfolio bank account. You almost always make more money by transitioning funds from your bank account into TIPS. The idea is to transfer your funds from your TIPS account into your other investments that yield more profit. The good news is that the TIPS referenced above are all highly liquid, especially through a brokerage like Robinhood. If you choose not to use a TIPS account as your cash reserve, and rather as a sole investment, I would only recommend allocating 5% of your assets into a TIPS. TIPS is not a good money maker, but it is a good spot to keep your excess funds secure. In the next chapter, we will uncover a successful portfolio structure that will assist you in making executive decisions to get your portfolio up and running. Are you ready to build a portfolio that sets you up for long-term wealth building? Let's begin.

PART III
A PORTFOLIO THAT BREEDS SUCCESS

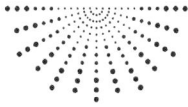

10

CRAFTING AN EXCEPTIONAL
PORTFOLIO

C ongratulations! You have successfully self-educated yourself about the endless opportunities to investing your money into the world's greatest economy. We have a lot to cover in this last chapter, but I assure you that you will be able to confidently invest by the end!

How can we predict the future? The simple answer, look into the statistics of the past. As stated in *The Little Book of Common Sense Investing*,

---

"Without exception every decade of significantly negative speculative return was immediately followed by a decade in which it turned positive by a correlative amount:
    the negative 1910s and then the roaring 1920s
    the dispiriting 1940s and then the booming 1950s
    the discouraging 1970s and the souring 1980s."

— JOHN BORGE

This is a remarkably brilliant observation when analyzing how to time the market, but I advise not attempting to time the market. Here is why. As stated in previous sections, total return investment averaged 9 percent from the 1900s to 2010. If you choose to invest long-term with a somewhat hands-off approach, the secret is as simple as three words. Buy and hold.

Lets give advanced investors the benefit of the doubt by saying to buy and hold as a strategy is vague and too simplistic for long-term wealth building. The ideology behind buying and holding is as follows. The goal is to diversify your portfolio to hold different investments. When the US dollar is weak, the price of gold and silver goes up. With a diversified portfolio, if you hold gold and silver, the best time to sell is when the US dollar is weak, and the price per ounce is at an all-time high. You can sell off some of your gold and silver then reinvest that sale into buying stocks that are currently trading at a low price. This is a good strategy because you are selling when the market is high and buying when other investments are on sale. This strategy has been coined *Asset Allocation*. Rebalancing your portfolio yearly gives you a big advantage to secure a higher ROI. Allocating your assets at the same time every year is an investor's shortcut to achieving financial wealth more quickly.

The money you make each year is irrelevant. Maybe thirty percent one year and perhaps only three percent the next. It all averages out in your favor if you buy and hold over the long-term of your life. We all have limited amounts of time on earth. The average lifespan of a man in the US is 78.6 years. A woman, 81.1 years. Imagine if you put the money you save into investments rather than a bank account. How much money does the bank pay you in interest? According to the FDIC, the national average interest rate for a savings account or a checking account is 0.06%. If you put $10,000 of your savings into a brokerage account, how much do you think you could make using the strategies listed in this book? I'll tell you how much you would make if you put that $10,000 into a savings or a checking account only making 0.06% interest. After one year, you would make $6 for leaving your money in the hands of a bank.

I hope you can see that investing in the market rather than at a bank is a no brainer when it comes to your money. Put your savings into a brokerage account and start making money every year by doing almost nothing. It's that easy, and that simple when you start.

High odds of success are attributed to investing long-term. Think of it like you are a cross country runner. You don't really care if you start the race slower than everyone else. There are so many miles/kilometers to run that you are focused on the end goal, which is finishing ahead of your competition. How do you finish first? I'm not sure, you'd have to ask a cross country runner. Although, I would assume the person who finishes first doesn't always have the fastest first lap. He/she has the discipline and understanding of long-term success. The same principle applies to investing in the stock market. Day trading and swing trading are a sure way to put you in first or last on any given day, but how about your long-term success? A day trader's goal is to run the fastest lap. There are many *get rich quick schemes* promoting how they have made millions day trading and they want to show you those secrets for a one time fee. Maybe they have a few good pointers but if their day trading model is as successful as these salesman proclaim, they would surely stick to making money from using their model instead of making their money by selling you a course for $999. You need a strategy for long-term success. Long-term investors understand the principle of patience and steady wealth building. Success, financial independence, and long-term wealth is achieved through hard work, you can not cheat the process.

We have had several talks on what to pick and what not to pick as investments through the stock market. I have no doubts that you listed your favorite stocks, and you are thinking of how to start. You undoubtedly understand that you have to research the investments that coincide with your goals. I hope you have found that the extensive research in this book can help you through your journey of achieving financial independence. But how do you begin investing, particularly from the comfort of your home?

Clearly, you have to understand how to get started in the stock market. I have dedicated this chapter to showing you the path to successfully starting your investment journey and creating your individual investment portfolio. I will illustrate a step by step guide to begin investing right from the comfort of your home.

To begin with, it may not be a sound idea to dump all your existing funds straight into the market. You need to have a feel of what the stock market offers if you are a beginner. You need to understand its interface, terms, structures, and tactics. You might fall into costly but straightforward errors that could be avoided if you take your time and learn more as you go.

All I'm saying is to start slow, get the ball rolling, and continue to educate yourself as opportunities present themselves.

"The power of hands-on learning is indisputable. But when it comes to investing your money in the stock market, however, making a beginner's mistakes can cost you more than just your self-esteem."

How do you avoid making a beginner's mistake? Have patience, make decisions based on data not emotion, and continue to self-educate yourself about the various opportunities offered through the stock market. Professional stockbrokers read and discover new things every day.

"Practice does not make perfect. It reduces imperfection."

— TUBA BETA

Nevertheless, you should learn to a point where you can satisfactorily delve into the market and make some good hits. You will certainly discover more as you get into actual practice.

Here is the solution for a cautious investor. Several online platforms have been created for you to get hands-on experience without investing your hard-earned money. Many of them are free, and several others are paid platforms. The free versions offer enough experience, so there really is no point in subscribing to paid versions, except perhaps, you find something spectacular. You would be confronted with a quasi-stock market situation (trades in real-time but you have virtual money). Basically, you get to invest fake funds into their software that tracks the market. You can see if you are successful or not successful. You will be provided with virtual cash and required to invest in various stocks. You can apply all the lessons taught in this book, as you would when you are in a real situation. So, this is going to be a lot of fun.

Recommendations

I have personally tried all the following, and I think they are top-notch. You should remember, the world is fast developing, and a viable alternative might be in the making. I have had a lot of personal experience with www.marketwatch. com/game/fet and their game simulator. For beginners looking to test the waters, this is an outstanding place to start. I still use their game system to try out any new strategies. As for an entire list of websites, they are as follows:

1. www.howthemoneymarketworks.com
2. www.youngmoney.com/stock-market-game
3. www.marketwatch.com/game/fet
4. www.wallstreetsurvivor.com
5. www.investopedia.com/simulator
6. www.updown.com

Some others are not simulators. They are investing websites that are specifically designed to help beginners. These companies offer advice. They also provide enough guidance to sail you through the beginning jitters. Many of them give you a free trial before full payment. Before signing up, read their expense costs. Company webpages include:

1. www.morningstar.com
2. www.zacks.com
3. www.seekingalpha.com
4. www.stockdvisors.com
5. www.barron's.com

Do you have to try all of them? Of course not! One site is enough to teach you the basics unless you feel the need to try more. Regardless, one or a few should be enough to teach you all you need to know.

- **Picking stocks**

When picking stocks, understand that simplistically, the price of a stock is based upon two variables at any point in time.

The goods or services the company sells.

Based on the company's performance, the stock price will go up or down. If Nike is having an amazing year of revenue and keeping their costs down, the stock price will probably go up because the company is doing well. Vice versa, if the company is underperforming, the stock price will go down.

As for the second reason, it's all about the hype.

As investors' expectations rise, there will be an increase in the *hype* around the stock fueling investors to buy. This increases the stock price too. Vice versa. If investors feel weary about the company's performance and start to sell their shares, the herd of sheep will follow and sell because of the hype revolving around the company is negative. The hype revolves all-around expectations and speculation while the first variable relies on last quarter's performance. Bogle says it perfectly here.

"My advice to investors: ignore the short-term sound and fury of the emotions reflected in our financial markets, and focus on the productive long-term economics of our corporate businesses."

— JOHN BOGLE

Let's get straight to business now. How do you venture into business as a stock investor? The following steps will guide you through successfully setting up a vibrant portfolio yourself.

Full Step By Step Process to Set Up an Investment Portfolio

Step 1: Set up an Online Brokerage Account

The first thing to do is set up an online brokerage account. You need to be recognized as a participant before you can play the real game as a participant. So, setting up your account is a sine qua non.

When setting up your account, you have a few factors to consider. These factors can help you trim down your options to what suits you and your investment goals. The four initiatives worth taking are as follows.

- **The type of brokerage account you'd like**

There are different types of investment plans. The type of brokerage account is referred to as an umbrella. Brokerage sites offer different packages too. Various plans provide various packages. The traditional method of investment, for example, does not offer a reduction in taxes. You would be charged when your dividends and fees are not tax-free, and you can pull out your funds the instant you are no longer interested. This may be ideal for you if you are saving to buy a home. Another option is an IRA, that is, Individual Retirement Account. A Roth IRA umbrella does not offer incentives if you take out funds before turning 59 and a half. But when you do turn 59 and a half the umbrella rewards you tremendously. If you are serious about long-term investing, a Roth IRA is a fantastic option. There are two things to note. You can take out the funds you have personally put in but not a single dollar of profit. If you liquidate any profits before age 59 and a half you will be penalized. Keep that in mind. There are at least ten types of umbrellas, but generally, they are tailored towards investing for the long-term future. I recommend long-term investing, as this was the inspiration behind the book and it greatly minimizes risk.

If you would rather invest in an individual brokerage account, taxes and fees apply, but your money is liquid, and you can access your funds around the clock. For example, if you want to take a trip around the world and pull out some of your funds, you would have to be 59 and a half with an IRA to pull out profits. With an individual brokerage account, you can take out any amount whenever you desire.

Your employer can directly fund an account like 403 (b), 401 (k), etc. If you are self-employed, a solo 401 (k) might be your suit too. It is impractically impossible to gather all the different types of brokerage accounts. There are so many different umbrellas, so research the one that suits your financial situation the best and the one that fits right into your timeline goals. Margin privileges, tax reduction, and instant access are among the few offers that I try to watch for. My professional recommendation would be a Roth IRA because of three reasons. Three reasons why Roth IRA's are supreme are tax-free withdrawals, tax-free growth, and no required minimum distributions.

- **Consider the cost**

The moment you make a list of the brokerage accounts that sound like "yeah, this is it", you will be faced with another obstacle. That is, how to select one of them based upon cost. You can ease out of these obstacles by paying attention to their general and hidden fees. You may want to spare some time to review their long-term costs too. The lower the expense rate, the higher the profit margin. The expense rate for every stock varies according to the company's wishes. For example, low-cost index funds track a broad portion of the market at a low expense rate. No matter what investments you choose, look at the expense ratio.

High Return - Low Expense = Win

- **Selecting your brokerage firm**

Next step is selecting a brokerage firm. You can do that online, of course. At some parts in this book, I have stressed that hiring a horrible manager is one of the worst errors anyone can ever make when investing. Therefore, you should thoroughly research and be doubly sure about a brokerage firm before approaching them. You are interested in their charge rate, records as a brokerage firm, ease of access, transparency, and reliability.

In the past, many brokerage firms had a minimum investment requirement and a fee attached to ever trade. I believe with Fidelity and E-Trade, every trade cost the investor $5. $5 is not a big deal to a big fish investor making a trade once a month but for the common small time investor making a few trades every month this can become costly. Thanks to Robinhood, small investors like you and I can trade on their platform for as little as $1 and no transaction fees. Today, many other brokerage sites have followed suit and canceled their policy of trade minimums and transaction fees. Fidelity and E-Trade no longer charge investors capital per trade.

Here are brokerage companies you can try out. They all have impressive records. As of 2020, they are considered the best for investors. In no particular order:

1. **TD AMERITRADE**
2. **E*TRADE**
3. **FIDELITY**
4. **ROBINHOOD**
5. **MERRIL EDGE**
6. **ACORN**
7. **CHARLES SCHWAB**
8. **ALLY INVEST**
9. **BETTERMENT**

For beginners, Robinhood is one of the best ways to get your foot in the door and start investing. I have Robinhood on my phone, and I have to tell you I couldn't be more pleased with its services. Starting with Robinhood gave me the confidence to explore other brokerage firms. Robinhood offers a simplistic approach for any investor who wants to get their feet wet while getting hands-on experience with full accessibility to the stock market. I find their brokerage service accessible and a more convenient version of going through your typical brokerage firm. You can track the progress of almost every stock and even make advanced trading moves like puts, calls, trailing stops, and more. With modern technology, Robinhood is the perfect set up for Millennials and Generation Z tech-savvy users. The best part, you can easily manage all of your investments 24/7 from the comfort of your cell phone. If you want to give Robinhood a try, use my referral code to receive a free stock like Apple, Ford, or Facebook!

https://join.robinhood.com/daniels13334

- **Fill out their application**

Research and select your preferred brokerage firm. Robinhood is simplistic while others can be more time consuming. Not to worry! After looking at the majority of these brokerage firms I will walk you through a typical process.

Go to their website and fill out their *New Account Application*. You would usually have to supply the necessary information like your name, location, social security number, and driver's license. Besides the tedious information, this phase is a walk in the park. Once your information is approved, you will have to fund the portfolio with some of the money you have saved. You can set up a monthly deposit or create your own strategy.

Step 2: **Select the Stocks You Want in Your Portfolio**

Now that you have an active portfolio through a brokerage firm, you need to fill it with stocks. I do not have to remind you that there are thousands of stocks on the market, and the investment options are relatively endless. Don't worry! We have touched on the many factors throughout the previous chapters, but I will summarize by listing three key elements. The factors you need to consider before selecting your investments are as follows.

- **Sector/Industry**

I would not advise investing in fine art stocks just because you have a fantasy of painting and things of that nature. You are here to make money. You want to choose the most promising sectors in the market. If you remember correctly, I hinted at the most profitable industries in one of the previous chapters. For convenience, I will reiterate that the two most promising sectors in 2020 are Technology and Bio-Tech.

- **Market type**

Depending on you risk/return beliefs, you can invest in large caps, mid-size caps, or small caps. Earlier, I have hinted that the best stocks you should invest in are stocks that pay high dividends. If you are someone in your 20's, you have decades to stack your dividends. It is miraculous how dividends and compound interest work wonders for an investment portfolio. You also remember that every stock charges a different rate to buy a share. The total number of shares you are buying will be determined by how much the share price is and how much you are willing to spend on that company.

- Ex. Apple Inc. (AAPL) 444.45 USD per Share.
- If your budget is $700, you have two options.

1. Buy in shares: 1 share of Apple Inc. at 444.45 USD
2. Buy in dollars: 1.57498… shares of Apple Inc. at 700 USD

- **Stock type**

From experience, I know that selecting the stock type is one of the easiest tasks you could ever engage in at this point because the previous steps can be much more tedious. All you have to do here is select a common or preferred stock. Remember, research and verify the dividend-paying record of a company before selecting its stocks. I will list the seven stock categories below for reference.

Blue Chip Stocks
Speculative Stocks
Growth Stocks
Value Stocks
Income Stocks
Penny Stocks
Cyclical Stocks

From Peter Lynch to Jack Bogle or Warren Buffett to Benjamin Graham, every large scale investor has their own unique opinion on which category is the most profitable.

There is statistical data supporting all of their individual opinions. It comes down to personal preference and more importantly, the portion of the market you understand the best. If you can spot a well performing ETF better than most people, don't invest in mutual funds because a guru on the internet tells you you're missing out. The fact is, there are an abundant amount of opportunities when investing in the stock market. *Keep the main thing the main thing* and stick to what you're good at.

Step 3: Setting up Your Stock Portfolio

When setting up your portfolio, weigh each investment with a precise percentage. Weighting is a technical term. Weighting refers to the science of adjusting the weight of the individual stocks that make up your portfolio. It is the habit of examining the percentage of each account so you could strike a balance between the weights of the stocks in your portfolio. For example, let's say you want 25% of your total investment in dividend-paying stocks, 20% in index funds that cover the market's spread, 20% in REITs, 20% in individual ETF stocks, 10% in mutual funds, and 5% in TIPS as a backbone diversification tool. This is an example of what weighing your portfolio looks like. A good strategy is to diversify your funds in percentages to track each investment's value and performance.

You are not lost by chance, are you? If you are, go through the lines again. You may like to consult the previous chapters where we discussed these terms if they seem awkward right now.

That said, you have to consider how to structure your portfolio to strike a balance that reflects your long-term aspirations. As the saying goes, there are a million ways to make a million dollars. To do that, you can diversify by investing in bonds, stocks, securities, etc. Diversification is a priority when creating your stock market portfolio to succeed in the long-term. Here are a few crucial tips to use when investing in each of them:

Stocks: Picking stocks, the market cap, the industry or sector, and the stock type are factors to be considered. Getting a Stock Screener can guide you through vital statistics of the stocks you are researching. Some Stock Screeners are free, and of course, others are not.

Bonds: When adding bonds to your portfolio, maturity is one of the most important factors to be considered. If it is a type of bond that would mature in a couple of years, it may not offer a lot of dividends, and it may not sound ideal to someone who desires to invest long-term. On the flip side, it might guide against inflation. It all depends on your research. Outside the maturity period, the dividends or coupons, and the credit rating are crucial factors. One last thing, you need to know whether you will be opting for TIPS or a traditional bond.

Mutual Funds: No doubt, mutual funds are among the most sought after investments. As with every other stock, expense cost is a factor you have to consider. You might want to research the feasibility of your fund manager's preferences if you go down the path of having someone else manage your money.

ETFs: If you are considering ETFs, it is a viable alternative to mutual funds, and they operate by similar caveats. You have to be certain the ETFs you are interested in, follow your investment goals and timeline. You also want to be doubly sure that you can achieve a balance between your investments.

Step 4: **Recurring Investments**

If investing was a game, It would arguably be life's most important game. How do you keep up with investing to where you don't have to constantly monitor your portfolio every day, week, or month? Recurring investments are a hands-off way you can stay investing without the hassle of consistently maintaining your stocks.

Invest monthly, quarterly, or yearly depending on your billing cycle or strategize purchasing when the market takes a drop (think of it as buying something on sale). Personally, my long-term investing plan would not work if I did not use recurring investments. The health of my portfolio depends on recurring investments.

If this interests you, send a direct deposit form from your brokerage to your bank, set the amount, and the funds will transfer from your bank account once a month into your portfolio. With a recurring investment, you automate your portfolio to your liking. Each month, my extra funds go into my Fidelity portfolio. I previously automated my portfolio to dispense the funds into my several accounts. This way, I can take a hands-off approach to building wealth. You don't have to constantly manage my portfolio or accounts because you can automate your portfolio to diversify funds automatically.

Let's talk low-cost index funds. I arrange all of my low-cost index funds into one account. I intend to buy and hold low-cost index funds every month. As time progresses, dividends compound and the market rises. You'll soon be amazed by the great feeling you'll have everyday knowing you are making money as you sleep.

Your account typically makes money for you during the day while you enjoy your life and at night when you sleep. Automate your portfolio to accept recurring investments, diversify the accepted funds in your financial accounts, and sit back and watch your money grow.

Below are three tiny steps for how to set up recurring investments.

1. Separate your investments using multiple accounts (ex. Roth IRA and Individual Brokerage) or one singular account. The account(s) will hold your investments under the umbrella of your entire portfolio.

2. Submit a direct deposit form to your bank detailing how much money you want to be transferred into your portfolio and how often (monthly, quarterly, or yearly). The direct deposit money from your bank goes straight into your cash reserve or buying power tab within your portfolio.

3. In your portfolio, diversify the funds from your cash reserve into your account(s) by dollar amount or by percentage. Example: cash reserve currently holds $1,000. We will use the example percentages from earlier (25% in dividend-paying stocks, 20% in index funds, 20% in REITs, 20% in ETFs, 10% in mutual funds, and 5% in TIPS). From the $1,000 in your cash reserve, you would automate your portfolio to automatically reinvest $250 in selected dividend stocks, $200 in index funds, $200 in REITs, $200 in ETFs, $100 in mutual funds, and $50 in TIPS.

When deciding how often you would like to invest, see the list below.

Let's say your budget is $2,400 a year.

1. Ex. $200 per month **x** 12 months = $2,400
2. Ex. $600 per quarter **x** 4 quarters = $2,400
3. Ex. $2,400 per year **x** 1 year = $2,400

Step 5: **Manage Your Portfolio**

It is more profitable to manage your own investment portfolio. Hiring helpers or fund managers are not necessary for you to build long-term wealth, and they might take away from your overall success. You are probably thinking, "How could a professional that is paid to help me actually hurt me?" In today's market, with the low expense costs of online brokerages, fund managers don't offer the incentives they used to. Princeton University professor and the author of *A Random Walk Down Wall Street* says,

---

"Experience conclusively shows that index fund buyers are likely to obtain results exceeding those of the typical fund manager, whose large advisory fees and substantial portfolio turnover tend to reduce investment yields.... The index fund is a sensible, serviceable method for obtaining the market's rate of return with absolutely no effort and minimal expense."

— BURTON G. MALKIEL

With the high commissions and the current time we live in, it is much better by all statistics that you manage your own stock portfolio. No one cares more about your money than you do. Plus, investing on your own takes away the high commissions investment managers charge.

Educate yourself to where you feel comfortable managing all of your stock options and investments by yourself. Successful investing is about owning businesses and reaping the rewards provided by dividends and earnings growth.

From the 1900's to 2010, the contribution of earnings growth to investment return averaged 4.6% per year. Total investment return (including dividends paid out to shareholders) averaged 9% per decade.

Sample Portfolio

In case there are some of you who had hoped for a specific "done for you investing model", you can find a sample portfolio at the end of this section.

Before I uncover the "done for you investing model", there are a few things to discuss.

The sample portfolio you are about to see is in no way a recommendation of how to build your individualized portfolio. We have already covered the 5 steps you should take to craft your new portfolio.

The people you went to high school with have vastly different financial habits and goals. As the cliche goes, *there are a million ways to make a million dollars.*

My portfolio will surely look different than yours because we have different investment goals. Take a long pause to think about your investment goals before diving into any investment. Make sure the investment that interests you aligns perfectly with your financial goals.

For instance, I thoroughly like high paying dividend stocks but I am willing to take a dividend cut for potential growth in stock price. To better explain this concept, let's look at two dividend paying investments.

- PowerShares S&P 500 High Dividend Low Volatility ETF **(SPHD)**

- Johnson and Johnson **(JNJ)**

Currently, **SPHD** pays an impressive dividend of 5.23 while **JNJ** pays a dividend of 2.64. On the surface, we see that **JNJ**'s dividend is about half of what **SPHD** pays out.

*What's the difference between **SPHD** and **JNJ**?*

SPHD has low volatility meaning the stock price doesn't increase or decrease dramatically over the long-term. In other words, the stock price is stagnant. Investing in this index for the next 20 years is a great investment but it is essential to understand that the money you will be making from **SPHD** will strictly be from dividend payments not stock growth.

JNJ on the other hand only pays half of the dividend **SPHD** pays but has more room for growth. Johnson and Johnson has been established for a long time and even through lawsuits, the company's stock price has shown positive growth. Investing in this stock for the next 20 years is a great investment because you will make money on an increase in stock price and dividend payments.

To predict which stock will make you more money in the next 20 years is like flipping a coin. There is no way to distinctively come to a conclusion because it comes down to unforeseen luck and your dedication to investing long-term.

After taking you the long way around the bar, I am ready to share with you my professional and personal investing portfolio. This portfolio is structured with diversity to ensure long-term success in any market. Here are 7 investments in your 20's that will change your life.

1. Dividend Paying Stock
Johnson and Johnson **(JNJ)**

2. S&P 500 Index Fund
Fidelity 500 Index Fund **(FXAIX)**

3. Nasdaq-100 Index Fund
Invesco QQQ Trust **(QQQ)**

4. Mutual Fund
Blackstone Group **(BX)**

5. Exchange Traded Fund
WisdomTree Emerging Markets High Dividend ETF **(DEM)**

6. Real Estate Investment Trust
Preferred Apartments Communities **(APTS)**

7. Treasury Inflation-Protected Security
SPDR Portfolio TIPS ETF **(SPIP)**

FINAL THOUGHTS: RESULTS THAT LAST A LIFETIME

I n drawing things to a close, I took some time to review the primary reason why I set out to write this book. I wanted to polish up the prospects of a bright future for young men and women. I hate to see older men and women living from hand to mouth, and I intensely hope that I am guiding you from it by writing this book. I long to make sure that young people have access to wealth-building techniques to enjoy the rest of their lives prosperously. From where I stand, we can all live an extraordinary life from now to the age when we feel no teeth in our buccal cavities. Take a second and imagine a world of older adults who didn't have to worry about medication, social security, and living expenses because they still have enough to cover everything and give to charity.

I am just an average man reporting proven techniques used by hedge fund managers, financial advisors, and market data compliance analysts. High school education never surfaced what it means to be an investor and how successful investors create significant ROI which funds their lifestyle. None of this information was disclosed in high school because, like myself, if the poor and middle class knew the right place to put their money, the wealth gap would be bridged. No longer will teens and 20-year-olds be misguided about where to put their money. My hopes are that the so-called *secret* was laid out simply, and you were able to soak up the information with ease.

After reading investment books and large textbooks that have aggressive formulas and complex definitions, I decided to put all of that Wall Street talk into an understandable book for someone in their 20's. How the economy effects the stock market is not simple, but successful investing has gotten a little easier for you.

From this day forward, you have the information, knowledge, and execution tactics to invest your money and most importantly change your life and the lives of your future family.

To accomplish that world, I have decided to share the methods I have applied in my life. Hopefully this gave you an insightful overview of the stock market. For young people who share the same dream for financial independence, it is achievable if you put your mind to it. This book has not only shown the way to achieve long-term financial success, but has also uncovered major shortcuts and industry secrets.

To steady this path, we spent the first couple of chapters stressing how vital it is to invest, with an emphasis on high paying dividends. I keenly hope you will target high paying dividends at all times because if you are in your 20's, time is your greatest ally.

In the next few chapters, we discussed index funds and

spoke about the S&P 500 index, while the Nasdaq-100 index followed. I extensively revealed how stable and promising these stocks are. Besides the Dow Jones, the S&P 500 and the Nasdaq-100 are next in line as the most reliable indexes of all time. Individual stocks have the potential to beat the market, but index funds give stable returns year after year without constant management of your portfolio.

You should not be surprised that each time we uncover a new investment, it seems to sound better than the previous one. Not only that, but it also looks better, more exciting, and much more appealing than the investment that came before it. This should not put you in a dilemma, however. The truth is that every investment you find in this book is reliable. They have made something of people who had nothing and merely struggled to live the lifestyle they desired. High paying dividend stocks, indexes, ETFs, mutual funds, REITs, and TIPS are all great for young men and women looking to expand their portfolio with diversification. Going full circle.

In the last chapter, I wrapped this book up with a step by step guide to help you venture into the most promising stock market in the world. I hope it is detailed and clear enough to get you started in the world of investing.

In my school of thoughts, you should lean towards the riskiest of these investments if you are in your early years. Equities, in particular, should hold a higher percentage of your portfolio. No one genuinely cares if a 20-year-old makes a mistake. Successful people fail hundreds of times before they succeed. With all of that said, I have to back my opinion with a stern advisory warning in the form of a universal rule. *Don't take stock advice from friends.* Conduct your own research to validate your reasons for investing. Reach out to your brokerage firm if you are unsure at any point. Successful investing is all about making decisions. To make executive decisions, you need to have confidence in your skills and abilities. If assertiveness and confidence is not a strong point in your personality, just know you will need it when making investing decisions.

Spectating is often easy because we are able to learn and take notes. The active investor transitions spectacles into action.

"The individual investor should act consistently as an investor and not as a speculator."

— BEN GRAHAM.

Let's be real, money doesn't grow on trees. I have had people ask me, "how do I invest money into the stock market when I feel like I have so little to spare?" Let's adopt Senator Elizabeth Warren's 50-30-20 budget rule. She advises that 50% of your life earnings should be spent on your basic needs. 30% should be spent on your casual desires, and reserving 20% to set yourself up for success (invest).

The final principle I will leave you with encapsulates the nature of investing for myself and hundreds of thousands of investors around the world. A principle of successful investing using baseball as an analogy.

When a baseball player steps into the batter's box, he is looking for the right opportunity to hit his *perfect pitch*. As a baseball player, he has seen thousands of pitches throughout his lifetime. He has seen bad pitches, good pitches, and every so often, the perfect pitch. The batter is able to distinguish the good from the bad most of the time, but it is truly remarkable when the batter is able to see the perfect pitch as the ball is coming out of the pitcher's hand. When he sees the perfect pitch, he swings and crushes the ball over the outfield wall.

So what does a baseball player seeing his perfect pitch have to do with investing? Warren Buffett explains this analogy further.

"They may be wonderful pitches to swing at, but if you don't know enough, you don't have to swing. And you can sit there and watch thousands of pitches and finally you get one right there where you want it ... and then you swing."

— WARREN BUFFETT

A successful baseball player is disciplined enough to know he can't swing at every pitch thrown his way. Investing is like baseball. There are over 2,500 companies listed on the stock market. In baseball, winners are selective with the pitches they swing at. In investing, winners are selective with the companies they invest in.

"I could improve your ultimate financial welfare by giving you a ticket with only 20 slots in it so that you had 20 punches representing all the investments that you got to make in a lifetime. And once you'd punched through the card, you couldn't make any more investments at all. Under those rules, you'd really think carefully about what you did and you'd be forced to load up on what you'd really thought about. So you'd do so much better."

— WARREN BUFFETT

Opportunities will come into your life at different times. You may receive an abundant amount of opportunities when you are not looking for any. On the flip side, you may be looking for any opportunity to come your way yet you are not receiving any. Be patient an have resilience.

As I stated in the last line of the introduction, if you are not willing to sacrifice for your goals, then your goals will become your sacrifice. I earnestly hope that I am able to meet your investment needs and show you some direction. I will be glad to read what you think of this book in the review section or through email.

I have taken a lot of energy to create a blueprint for 20-year-old's that model financial success. Unsurprisingly, I took a very long break from work, friends, and even family to create this guide to help bridge the wealth gap.

Should you get confused at any point or any topic, you should be sure you can reach me. Politely drop a question, and I assure you that my answer will be prompt in as little time as possible. You can reach me at my website danbusinesslifestyle.com or you can directly shoot me an email at dan@danbusinesslifestyle.com. I wish you a thrilling business in the stock market.

HOW TO APPLY THESE IDEAS TO BUSINESS

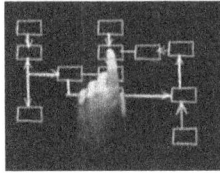

Taking care of your mindset is one of the most natural ways to propel yourself forward. Diving headfirst into our goals takes discipline. It is our choice to create outcomes that take from us or outcomes that pay us back. I've compiled many of the most practical long-term investments into a bonus chapter based on a Nobel Prize-winning strategy. I think you will discover it to be a staggeringly helpful expansion to the main ideas referenced in *7 Investments In Your 20's That Will Change Your Life.*

You can access the Bonus Chapter for free through my website. Go to the Articles tab then click Bonus Chapter.

danbusinesslifestyle.com

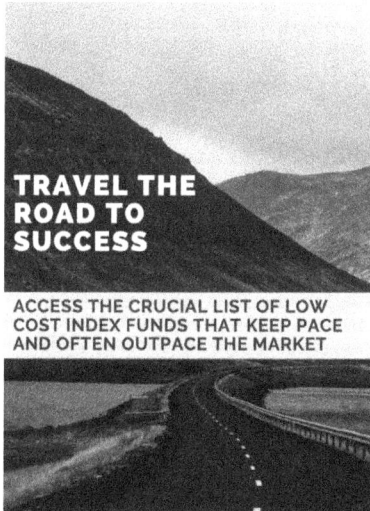

TRAVEL THE ROAD TO SUCCESS

ACCESS THE CRUCIAL LIST OF LOW COST INDEX FUNDS THAT KEEP PACE AND OFTEN OUTPACE THE MARKET

Free Gift to Readers

Access the exclusive list of the nine lowest cost index funds backed by Vanguard, Fidelity, and others. You don't want to miss out on these nine blue-chip investments! Visit the link below to get yours instantly.

https://danbusinesslifestyle.activehosted.com/f/5

NOTES

1. "100 Index." Nasdaq. https://www.nasdaq.com/nasdaq-100.
2. "5 Best Index Funds In October 2020 | Bankrate." Google. https://www.google.com/amp/s/www.bankrate.com/investing/best-index-funds/amp/.
3. "5 REIT Investing Mistakes To Avoid | Bankrate." Google. https://www.google.com/amp/s/www.bankrate.com/investing/reit-investing-mistakes-to-avoid/amp/.
4. "ACCOUNT CENTER." Individual - Cashing Paper Savings Bonds. https://www.treasurydirect.gov/indiv/research/indepth/bond-redeem.htm.
5. "Actively Managed ETFs." ETFdb.com. https://etfdb.com/themes/actively-managed-etfs/.
6. Admin. Warren Buffet on Investment. May 31, 2016. https://warrenbuffettoninvestment.com/warren-buffetts-best-advice-on-successful-investing/.

7. Admin. Warren Buffet on Investment. February 12, 2018. http://warrenbuffettoninvestment.com/.

8. Amadeo, Kimberly. "Don't Buy TIPS Until You Read This." The Balance. https://www.thebalance.com/what-are-treasury-inflation-protected-securities-3306098.

9. Amadeo, Kimberly. "What the S&P 500 Tells You About America's Health." The Balance. https://www.thebalance.com/what-is-the-sandp-500-3305888.

10. Authors Nasdaq Global Indexes MarketInsite. "When Performance Matters: Nasdaq-100 vs. S&P 500 First Quarter '20." Nasdaq. https://www.nasdaq.com/articles/when-performance-matters:-nasdaq-100-vs.-sp-500-2020-04-24.

11. Authors Nasdaq Global Indexes MarketInsite. "Why Millennials Are Gravitating to the Nasdaq-100." Nasdaq. https://www.nasdaq.com/articles/why-millennials-are-gravitating-to-the-nasdaq-100-2020-05-08.

12. Backman, Maurie. "A Cat Outperformed Pro Stock-Pickers. Here's What That Means for Investors." The Motley Fool. August 01, 2016. https://www.fool.com/investing/2016/08/01/a-cat-outperformed-pro-stock-pickers-heres-what-th.aspx.

13. Beattie, Andrew. "A Quick Guide for Futures Quotes." Investopedia. August 28, 2020. https://www.investopedia.com/articles/active-trading/011515/quick-guide-futures-quotes.asp.

14. Benson, Alana Is One of NerdWallet's Investing Writers. She Is the Author of "Data Personified.

"Types of Real Estate Investments." NerdWallet. September 02, 2020. https://www.nerdwallet. com/blog/investing/types-of-real-estate-investments/.

15. Bloomenthal, Andrew. "How Can I Buy an S&P 500 Fund?" Investopedia. September 10, 2020. https://www.investopedia.com/ask/answers/how-can-i-buy-sp-500-fund/.

16. Bogle, John C. *The Little Book of Common Sense Investing: The Only Way to Guarantee Your Fair Share of Stock Market Returns (Anniversary, Revised, Updated)*. Wiley, 2017.

17. "Business Money Market Savings Account." Money Market Savings Account | Money Market Funds | Santander Bank. https://www.santanderbank. com/us/en/business/banking/checking-savings/money-market-savings.

18. Caplinger, Dan. "Nasdaq 100 Index Fund: What You Need to Know." The Motley Fool. June 19, 2017. https://www.fool.com/amp/investing/2017/06/19/nasdaq-100-index-fund-what-you-need-to-know.aspx.

19. Chen, James. "Bond ETF Definition." Investopedia. August 29, 2020. https://www.investopedia.com/terms/b/bond-etf.asp.

20. Chen, James. "Consumer Price Index (CPI) Definition." Investopedia. August 28, 2020. https://www.investopedia.com/terms/c/consumerpriceindex.asp.

21. Chen, James. "Exchange Traded Fund - " ETFs." Investopedia. September 28, 2020. https://www.investopedia.com/terms/e/etf.asp.

22. Chen, James. "Exploring the Benefits and Risks of Inverse ETFs." Investopedia. August 29, 2020. https://www.investopedia.com/terms/i/inverse-etf.asp.

23. Chen, James. "Real Estate Definition." Investopedia. September 09, 2020. https://www.investopedia.com/terms/r/realestate.asp.

24. Chen, James. "Real Estate Investment Group." Investopedia. September 16, 2020. https://www.investopedia.com/terms/r/reig.asp.

25. Chen, James. "Real Estate Investment Trust (REIT) Definition." Investopedia. August 28, 2020. https://www.investopedia.com/terms/r/reit.asp.

26. Chen, James. "Should You Be Open to a Closed-End Fund?" Investopedia. September 16, 2020. https://www.investopedia.com/terms/c/closed-endinvestment.asp.

27. Chen, James. "Stock Screener." Investopedia. August 29, 2020. https://www.investopedia.com/terms/s/stockscreener.asp.

28. Chen, James. "Technical Analysis of Stocks and Trends." Investopedia. September 25, 2020. https://www.investopedia.com/terms/t/technical-analysis-of-stocks-and-trends.asp.

29. Chen, James. "Treasury Inflation-Protected Securities Protect Investors From Inflation." Investopedia. September 22, 2020. https://www.investopedia.com/terms/t/tips.asp.

30. Chen, James. "What Is a Commodity ETF?" Investopedia. September 16, 2020. https://www.investopedia.com/terms/c/commodity-etf.asp.

31. Clark, Ken. "Where to Find a List of the Stocks in

the S&P 500." Investopedia. October 05, 2020. https://www.investopedia.com/ask/answers/08/find-stocks-in-sp500.asp.

32. Contributor Prableen Bajpai. "How and Why to Invest in the Nasdaq-100 Index." Nasdaq. https://www.nasdaq.com/articles/how-and-why-to-invest-in-the-nasdaq-100-index-2020-03-20.

33. Cussen, Mark P. "The Basics of REIT Taxation." Investopedia. October 02, 2020. https://www.investopedia.com/articles/pf/08/reit-tax.asp.

34. Dennis Publishing Ltd. "The Former Factory Worker Who Predicted the Digital Age." The Week, no. 1085, Aug. 2016, p. 36.

35. "Elderly Poverty Statistics - Economic Security." NCOA. September 04, 2020. https://www.ncoa.org/news/resources-for-reporters/get-the-facts/economic-security-facts/.

36. "Equities Price List: The Nigerian Stock Exchange." Equities Price List | The Nigerian Stock Exchange. http://www.nse.com.ng/market-data/trading-statistics/equities.

37. "Features of Exchange Traded Funds (ETF)." IndianMoney. https://indianmoney.com/articles/features-of-exchange-traded-funds---etf.

38. Gallant, Chris. "Learn 4 Steps to Building a Profitable Portfolio." Investopedia. August 29, 2020. https://www.investopedia.com/financial-advisor/steps-building-profitable-portfolio/.

39. Gordon Scott, CMT. "Futures Exchange Definition." Investopedia. September 16, 2020. https://www.investopedia.com/terms/f/futuresexchange.asp.

40. "Harmony Quotes (854 Quotes)." Goodreads. https://www.goodreads.com/quotes/tag/harmony.

41. Hayes, Adam. "Mutual Fund Definition." Investopedia. August 28, 2020. https://www.investopedia.com/terms/m/mutualfund.asp#understanding-mutual-funds.

42. Holker, Allison. "Allison Holker's Top 10 Reasons to Go for It." Dance Spirit, vol. 19, no. 7, Dance Media LLC, dba Macfadden Performing Arts Media, LLC, Sept. 2015, p. 80.

43. Home. http://www.krammerfinancial.com/.

44. "How to Build an Investment Portfolio." U.S. News & World Report. https://money.usnews.com/investing/investing-101/articles/how-to-build-an-investment-portfolio.

45. "Inflation Quotes." BrainyQuote. https://www.brainyquote.com/topics/inflation-quotes.

46. Investopedia. "Real Estate Investing." Investopedia. September 16, 2020. https://www.investopedia.com/mortgage/real-estate-investing-guide/.

47. "It Is Only through Labor and Painful Effort, by Theodore Roosevelt." Daily Inspiration. http://www.inspiration-daily.com/said/only-through-labor-painful-effort-136/.

48. Jason. "50 Inspirational Real Estate Investment Quotes To Keep You Motivated." Property Management Dallas Forth Worth, TX. April 20, 2018. https://www.leapdfw.com/blog/inspirational-quotes-for-real-estate-investors/.

49. "Jim Rohn Quote: "The Rich Invest Their Money and Spend What Is Left; the Poor Spend Their

Money and Invest What Is Left."" Quotefancy.
https://quotefancy.com/quote/837661/Jim-Rohn-
The-rich-invest-their-money-and-spend-what-is-
left-the-poor-spend-their-money.

50. KenFaulkenberry. "What Is an ETF? Advantages &
Disadvantages." Arbor Asset Allocation Model
Portfolio (AAAMP) Value Blog. May 01, 2019.
https://www.arborinvestmentplanner.com/what-
is-an-etf-advantages-disadvantages-newsletter/.

51. Kennon, Joshua. "The 8 Different Types of Real
Estate Investments for New Investors." The
Balance. https://www.thebalance.com/different-
types-of-real-estate-investments-you-can-make-
357986.

52. Kennon, Joshua. "Here Are Some Tips on Building
a Complete Financial Portfolio." The Balance.
https://www.thebalance.com/building-complete-
financial-portfolio-357968.

53. Kenton, Will. "S&P 500 Index." Investopedia.
September 08, 2020. https://www.investopedia.
com/terms/s/sp500.asp.

54. Kenton, Will. "Weighted." Investopedia. September
16, 2020. https://www.investopedia.com/
terms/w/weighted.asp.

55. Kessler, Sarah. "5 Great Games for Learning Stock
Market Strategy." Mashable. October 22, 2010.
https://mashable.com/2010/10/22/stock-market-
games/.

56. Majaski, Christina. "What Is the Difference
Between an ETF and a Mutual Fund?"
Investopedia. October 02, 2020. https://www.

investopedia.com/articles/investing/110314/key-differences-between-etfs-and-mutual-funds.asp.

57. Matt Frankel, CFP. "Investing in REITs 101: The Pros and Cons." Millionacres. September 10, 2020. https://www.fool.com/millionacres/real-estate-investing/reits/reit-investing-101/.

58. Mauzy, Stephen. "Your Exchange-Traded Fund (ETF) Is Riskier Than You Think." Wyatt Investment Research. September 16, 2015. https://www.wyattresearch.com/article/exchange-traded-fund-etf-risk/.

59. Maxwell, John C. *How Successful People Think: Change Your Thinking, Change Your Life*. Center Street, 2009.

60. Merritt, Cam. "What Are the Differences Between the Dow Jones, NASDAQ & S&P 500?" Finance. March 05, 2019. https://finance.zacks.com/differences-between-dow-jones-nasdaq-sp-500-5513.html.

61. Money Management Quotes. https://www.personalfinancequotes.com/cat/moneymanagement1.htm.

62. "Mutual Funds Quotes." BrainyQuote. https://www.brainyquote.com/topics/mutual-funds-quotes.

63. "NASDAQ Full Form - Javatpoint." Www.javatpoint.com. https://www.javatpoint.com/nasdaq-full-form.

64. Ndimele, Uche. "The Pain and Gain of Money Market Fund Investment." Nairametrics. July 02, 2019. https://nairametrics.com/2019/07/02/the-pain-and-gain-of-money-market-fund-

investment/.

65. Online Trading with Smart Investment App. https://capital.com/amp/nasdaq-100-vs-sp-500.

66. Otman, Rob. "Six Long-Term Dividend Stocks for Income Investors." Investment U. September 22, 2020. https://investmentu.com/long-term-dividend-stocks/.

67. Pareto, Cathy. "Mutual Fund vs. ETF: What's the Difference?" Investopedia. August 28, 2020. https://www.investopedia.com/articles/exchangetradedfunds/08/etf-mutual-fund-difference.asp.

68. Petroff, Eric. "Introduction to Treasury Inflation-Protected Securities (TIPS)." Investopedia. August 28, 2020. https://www.investopedia.com/investing/introduction-treasury-inflation-protected-securities-tips/.

69. "Practice Quotes (481 Quotes)." Goodreads. https://www.goodreads.com/quotes/tag/practice.

70. "Quote from Benjamin Franklin." The Quotations Page. http://www.quotationspage.com/quote/2897.html.

71. "Real Estate Crowdfunding Platforms: Property Crowdfunding." P2P Lending | Crowdlending. June 25, 2020. https://crowdfunding-platforms.com/real-estate-crowdfunding.

72. Reinkensmeyer, Blain. "5 Best Online Brokers for Beginners 2020." StockBrokers.com. September 28, 2020. https://www.stockbrokers.com/guides/beginner-investors.

73. Robinson, Paul, and Strategist. "Difference between Dow, Nasdaq, and S&P 500: Major Facts

& Opportunities." DailyFX. https://www.dailyfx.
com/dow-jones/differences-between-dow-
nasdaq-and-sp-500.html/amp.

74. Rowley, Jason D. "A Beginner's Dictionary of
Venture Capital." Mattermark. June 23, 2017.
https://mattermark.com/venture-capital-
dictionary/.

75. Royal, James. "How to Buy Bonds: A Step-by-Step
Guide for Beginners." NerdWallet. February 12,
2019. https://www.nerdwallet.com/blog/
investing/how-to-buy-bonds/.

76. Royal, James. "The Nasdaq Index May Be Riskier
Than You Think." NerdWallet. April 12, 2018.
https://www.nerdwallet.com/blog/investing/
nasdaq-100-index-risks/.

77. "The S&P 500: A Dividend Yield & Growth
Overview." Dividend.com. https://www.dividend.
com/how-to-invest/the-sp-500-a-dividend-
overview/.

78. "SPY Interactive Stock Chart | SPDR S&P 500 ETF
Trust Stock." Yahoo! Finance. https://finance.
yahoo.com/chart/SPY.

79. Scott, Gordon. "Heavy Hitters Drive Nasdaq 100
Performance." Investopedia. September 12, 2020.
https://www.investopedia.com/heavy-hitters-
4776864.

80. Segal, Troy. "Fundamental Analysis." Investopedia.
August 28, 2020. https://www.investopedia.com/
terms/f/fundamentalanalysis.asp.

81. Serena Kappes Is a Veteran Journalist. "How to
Invest in the S&P 500 Index." Acorns. https://

www.acorns.com/money-basics/how-to-invest-in-the-sandp-500-index/.

82. Service, IIFL News. "Important Factors to Consider Before Choosing Mutual Fund." IIFL - India Infoline. November 24, 2017. https://www.indiainfoline.com/article-amp/news-personalfinance/important-factors-to-consider-before-choosing-mutual-fund-117112400449_1.html.

83. Study.com. https://study.com/academy/lesson/types-of-treasury-securities-definition-characteristics.html.

84. "A Tale of Two Indices - Nasdaq 100 vs S&P 500: FundsIndia Blog." Insights. May 05, 2020. https://www.fundsindia.com/blog/mf-research/a-tale-of-two-indices-nasdaq-100-vs-sp-500/18575.

85. "Treasury-securities-definition: Dictionary of Financial Terms:." TheStreet. https://www.thestreet.com/topic/47281/treasury-securities.html.

86. Tretina, Kat. "Best Retirement Plans For You." Forbes. September 17, 2020. https://www.forbes.com/sites/davidrae/2018/07/23/10-retirement-accounts-you-should-know-about/.

87. "Unrivaled Performance." Daily Stock Market Overview, Data Updates, Reports & News. https://www.nasdaq.com/Nasdaq-100/performance.

88. Voigt, Kevin, and Kevin Voigt Kevin Voigt Is a Personal Finance Writer at NerdWallet. He Has Covered Financial Issues for 20 Years. "What Are the Different Types of Mutual Funds?" NerdWallet. June 03, 2020. https://www.nerdwallet.com/blog/

investing/what-are-the-different-types-of-mutual-funds.

89. The Wall Street Journal. https://guides.wsj.com/personal-finance/investing/how-to-choose-an-exchange-traded-fund-etf/.

90. "Wilmington Large-Cap Strategy Fund." Citywire. https://citywireusa.com/professional-buyer/fund/wilmington-large-cap-strategy-fund-institutional/c103489?periodMonths=36.

91. Yochim, Dayana. "Index Funds: How to Invest and Best Funds to Choose." NerdWallet. October 06, 2020. https://www.nerdwallet.com/article/investing/how-to-invest-in-index-funds.

92. Zach Is the Author behind Four Pillar Freedom. "S&P 500 vs. Nasdaq 100: Which Index Is Better?" Four Pillar Freedom. October 21, 2019. https://fourpillarfreedom.com/sp-500-vs-nasdaq-100-which-index-is-better/.